contents

ULTIMATE
budget
cookbook

EDITED BY
MICHELE SIMMONS

© 2004 Caxton Editions

This edition published 2004 by
Caxton Editions an imprint of
The Caxton Publishing Group Ltd
20 Bloomsbury Street
London WC1B 3JH

Design and compilation by
The Partnership Publishing Solutions Ltd **www.the-pps.co.uk**

Printed and bound in Singapore

healthy nutritious meals on a budget

It's no secret that we should all be trying to eat healthier but it can seem a tall order when you're buying, and cooking, on a budget. The good news is that lack of funds doesn't have to mean a lack of goodness when it comes to food for the family. The key is know-how – which is exactly where the *Ultimate Budget Cookbook* comes in.

On the following pages you'll discover how everyone can eat healthily – and well – with our selection of over one hundred meals to choose from. So, whether you're a student away from home, or a mum trying to turn a few basics into a banquet, this book is full of surprises – and none of them costs a fortune!

getting basic…

Most people have a few basic utensils in their cupboards but we think it also helps if you have some of the following. Many you may have, or in some cases it'll be something similar, which is fine. But just in case you don't, here are what we consider are some budget essentials!

- colander and sieve
- measuring jug, ideally with both imperial and metric measurements
- measuring spoons
- chopping boards – keep a separate one for raw meat
- grater
- heavy-based large all-purpose frying pan
- saucepans, ideally three – small, medium and large
- roasting tin
- casserole and pie dishes
- flan dishes for quiches and tarts
- selection of cake and flan tins
- sharp knives including bread knife, carving knife, and general all-purpose one for filleting as well as chopping
- knife sharpener
- scales, ideally with both metric and imperial measurements
- selection of mixing bowls
- lemon squeezer
- garlic press
- spatulas
- vegetable peeler, slotted spoon, carving fork, apple corer, masher, ladle, serving spoons

- timer

- balloon whisk

- electric mixer, either free standing or hand-held

- wooden spoons

- kitchen foil, parchment paper, clingfilm.

measuring up

Our recipes include both metric and imperial measurements. Use whichever you're more comfortable with but make sure you stick to just one of them.

Other useful conversions which are worth knowing are:

3 tsp	=	1 tablespoon
1 oz jam, golden syrup or treacle	=	1 tablespoon
1 oz sugar	=	2 tablespoons
half ounce flour	=	2 tablespoons

With all the recipes take into account that oven temperatures can differ and you may need to adjust times and heat according to manufacturers' instructions.

solids

metric	imperial
15 g	$1/2$ oz
30 g	1 oz
60 g	2 oz
90 g	3 oz
120 g	4 oz ($1/4$ lb)
150 g	5 oz
180 g	6 oz
240 g	8 oz ($1/2$ lb)
360 g	12 oz ($3/4$ lb)
480 g	16 oz (1 lb)

ULTIMATE
budget cookbook

liquids

metric	imperial	american (cups)
15 ml	$1/2$ fl oz	1 tbsp
30 ml	1 fl oz	$1/8$ cup
60 ml	2 fl oz	$1/4$ cup
90 ml	3 fl oz	$3/8$ cup
125 ml	4 fl oz	$1/2$ cup
150 ml	5 fl oz ($1/4$ pint)	$2/3$ cup
175 ml	6 fl oz	$3/4$ cup
250 ml	8 fl oz	1 cup
300 ml	10 fl oz ($1/2$ pint)	$1^1/4$ cups
375 ml	12 fl oz	$1^1/2$ cups
500 ml	16 fl oz	2 cups
600 ml	20 fl oz (1 pint)	$2^1/2$ cups
900 ml	$1^1/2$ pints	$3^3/4$ cups
1 litre	$1^3/4$ pints	1 quart
$1^1/4$ litres	2 pints	$1^1/4$ quarts
2 litres	$3^1/4$ pints	2 quarts

oven temperatures

^oC	^oF	gas mark
110	225	$1/4$
120	250	$1/2$
140	275	1
150	300	2
160	325	3
175	350	4
190	375	5
200	400	6
220	425	7
230	450	8
240	475	9
260	500	10

storecupboard essentials

These are the convenience items that tend to be used every day. Generally what you have in your cupboard is down to personal taste but there are some foods that apart from being in constant use – for example salt and pepper – can also add a little inexpensive excitement to a dish and work wonders on the taste buds! What's more, having them handy means you can always whip up a 'little something' whether it's for unplanned guests or a hungry member of the family! And the best part is that by using a selection of the following foods we can guarantee that you'll have food on the table that's been easy to prepare, is inexpensive – and tastes great!

Apart from salt and pepper, our suggestions include:

- selection of dried herbs and spices
- stock cubes
- pasta
- rice
- soy sauce
- mustard
- ketchup
- tomato purée
- passata
- flour
- sugar
- eggs
- garlic
- oil
- vinegar.

ULTIMATE
budget cookbook

A selection of tinned products such as:

- tomatoes

- baked beans

- kidney beans

- tuna

- mackerel

- sardines

- sweetcorn

- fruit.

the best of health...

Although talking about healthy eating is nothing new these days you can, at times, be forgiven for wondering what all the fuss is about. In fact, though, eating healthily can be one of the most important ways to not only help ourselves feel well, but be well too. But opting for healthier choices doesn't mean increasing your food bill, cutting back on taste – or on all your favourite foods. It's just a matter of making some simple changes and making sure that you try to balance what you eat. Healthy eating is about eating foods that are rich in vitamins and minerals and provide the maximum nutrients that our bodies need to keep them in peak condition. What we've tried to prove in this book is that it is possible to eat healthily – and stay within budget. The key is knowing what *are* the healthier options. Once you know that, you can plan your meals accordingly.

In fact, there's no single food that provides all the nutrients we need, in the amounts we need them, which is why it's important to eat a mixture of foods. We all need to get a good mixture of proteins (fish, meat and cheese or vegetable sources such as pulses and cereals), carbohydrates (bread and pasta, preferably the unrefined sort) and fruit and vegetables.

The main part of our diet should be made up of starchy foods like bread, rice, pasta, cereals, potatoes and yams. These foods are particularly good news as they're filling because they're high in fibre, they're low in fat and they also contain vitamins and minerals. It's also important you get plenty of vegetables and fruit. Experts recommend you aim for between five and nine portions a day. But that's not as difficult to achieve as it sounds when you think that one portion is just two tablespoons of vegetables (fresh or frozen), or a small salad, two tablespoons of cooked or tinned fruit, a small carton of fruit juice and, of course, a piece of fruit. Another food group that's important to include in your diet is cheese and milk products which are rich in calcium and so important for strong bones for all the family. And you can opt for the low-fat versions (for example, low-fat yoghurts, margarines etc) which have just as much calcium, protein and B vitamins.

Also important in the diet – but in smaller quantities – is meat and other protein alternatives such as poultry, fish, pulses (beans, lentils, dried beans), eggs and nuts. The last food group in our dietary cocktail is the fatty and sugary foods which are the biscuits, cakes, chocolate, cream, crisps, pastry, savoury snacks, soft and alcoholic drinks, sugar and sweets. This should form the smallest part of the nutritional cocktail though the temptation can be that this becomes one of the greatest – even when you don't realise it! Although all of these foods may contain some useful nutrients they are also full of fat, sugar and salt – all of which are not such good news for our health. So, all need to be eaten in small quantities – if at all!

the fats of life…

While fat is an essential part of the diet – none of us needs very much of it. The problem is that many of the fats we eat are hidden so even when we're trying to cut back, it can be difficult to do! As well as many of the foods listed above, large quantities of fat are also found in products like sausages, burgers, chips, pies, gravies, salamis, luncheon meats, pastries and puddings – often the very foods that come under the heading 'family favourites'!

The real problem with fat, besides the fact that it's contained in so many processed products, is that eating too much of it can increase your risk of heart disease. And here in the UK we top the list of the countries that suffer the highest rate of the disease. Eating a high-fat diet has also been linked to some cancers – including breast and bowel cancer. Experts have also found that it can increase your risk of a number of conditions from diabetes to obesity. While of course there is a hereditary factor in many conditions, a high-fat diet can significantly increase your risk of developing those conditions – as can smoking and a sedentary lifestyle.

While experts recommend that we reduce our overall level of fat intake, the fat in food is often a mixture of three kinds: saturated fats, mono-unsaturates and polyunsaturates.

Saturated fats are found in animal foods but can also be made by hardening vegetable fats to make processed foods and hard margarines. Fats that are hard contain the most saturates and it's these that increase the level of cholesterol in the blood – which raises the risk of heart disease. Polyunsaturated fats are found in vegetable oils and plant foods. These are thought to help lower blood cholesterol levels as well as containing essential fatty acids which can't be made by the body. Monosaturated fats are found in olive oil and rapeseed oil, plus some nuts and vegetables. While they are not thought to specifically raise cholesterol levels, they seem ineffective in terms of lowering it.

To cut back on fat try some of the following:

- Trim the fat off meat when you can.

- Eat more poultry and fish – which is lower in fat – and lean meat.

- Fry food occasionally rather than regularly and then use oils rather than hard fats.

- Where you can, opt for lower-fat alternatives whether it means going for skimmed or semi-skimmed milk or low-fat yoghurts, sausages or prepared foods.

- Fill up on bread, cereals, potatoes, fruit and vegetables.

- Beware of invisible fats in foods like biscuits, cakes, chocolate, pastry and savoury snacks.

- When in doubt, check labels. If fat, and saturated fat in particular, is near the top on the list of ingredients then chances are you're looking at a high-fat food.

the sweet truth...

Although sugar gives us energy, too much sugar can cause a general excess energy intake which can, in turn, cause obesity. What's more, as sugar contains only calories but no significant nutrients, when you eat any food that is high in sugar, essentially you're getting the calories without the goodness. So while your calorie intake zooms up, your vitamin and mineral intake remains at zero. Also, you do get energy from other foods but, unlike with sugar-rich choices, you don't increase the risk of other problems like tooth decay.

To cut back on sugary foods, try some of the following:

- If you're buying soft drinks, choose low-calorie ones or unsweetened fruit juices diluted with water or soda.

- Buy tinned fruit canned in juice rather than in syrup.

- Try halving the sugar in recipes – it works for most things except jam, meringues and ice-cream.

- Cut down on jam, marmalade, honey, syrup and treacle.

- Use low-sugar or reduced-sugar varieties of everyday foods.

- Choose wholegrain cereals rather than those coated with honey.

- Go easy on cakes, biscuits, burfi and all kinds of sweet pastries and restrict the amount of sweets, chocolate and cereal bars.

- If you can't get used to drinks without sweetness, try using artificial sweeteners.

ULTIMATE
budget cookbook

filling up not filling out…

One very good way of making sure that the balance of your diet is right is to include plenty of fibre-rich foods like cereals, grains, oats, oat bran, seeds, beans, peas, vegetables and fruit. The fibre in these foods is thought to help to reduce the amount of cholesterol in the blood. Other high-fibre foods include wholemeal bread, wholemeal pasta and brown rice. These fibre-rich foods are also good news because not only do they help prevent constipation, they also contain more vitamins and minerals and, as they tend to have more bulk than fibre free foods, it means they fill you – so you're unlikely to overeat. Fibre in the diet is also thought to reduce the risk of developing diseases of the bowel, from bowel cancer to diverticulitis, as well as helping to lower our cholesterol levels and the level of sugar in the blood for diabetics. And it's worth knowing that it can also work wonders for anyone who suffers from more common conditions like constipation and haemorrhoids!

To increase the amount of fibre you eat, try some of the following:

• Eat a variety of fruit and vegetables every day.

• Use wholemeal flour rather than white flour when baking – or try half white and half wholemeal.

• Include baked beans in your diet – they're a cheap and easy way of getting fibre into your diet.

• Use more peas, lentils and beans, whenever you can. They're cheap as well as being highly nutritious.

salt

One last word on healthy eating. Go easy on the salt. It can cause high blood
pressure which, in turn, increases the risk of heart disease, as well as strokes.
A good way of cutting down is by adding less salt to cooking – use herbs and
spices for seasoning – and to leave the salt cellar off the table! Another easy
way of cutting down is to simply buy less of salty foods like bacon, cheese,
snacks, convenience foods, pickles and smoked fish.

ULTIMATE
budget cookbook

cutting the cost...

Although we've already said that it pays to plan ahead when you're deciding which meals to cook it also pays to take advantage of special offers — whether they're foods that you can buy in bulk and store or ones that are equally easy to freeze. So the secret is to have a plan — but be flexible with it!

- Opt for family-sized packets where you can — they work out much cheaper.

- Using lentils and dried pulses makes meat go further.

- In fruit dishes, where you can always use seasonal fruits, even if it means substituting the fruit given in the recipes.

- Buy an all-purpose polyunsaturated margarine rather than more expensive low-fat spreads which often can't be used for cooking.

- Look out for local markets which often sell produce cheaper than at the supermarket — particularly at the end of the day when they want to get rid of that day's stock!

- Cut out money-off coupons from papers and magazines when you see them, then put them in your purse — that way you'll remember to look out for that month's special offers.

- Save vegetable trimmings for soups and turn soups into complete meals by adding pasta and lentils or other pulses and grains.

- If you can, buy sacks of potatoes and trays of eggs from a local grower or farm shop.

- Make several meals vegetable-based ones — they're cheaper than meat and fish and are often healthier, too!

- Try to leave children at home when you're out shopping — that way you won't be talked into buying those little 'extras', like bags of sweets and bars of chocolate, that you hadn't budgeted for...

the recipes…

Although called starters these recipes can easily be used when you're looking for something to fill the gap. There are also soups included. They're not only simple to make, but they are also good news nutritionally so you really can end up dishing up a bowl full of goodness. Served with a chunk of bread they can be a meal in themselves and in the winter there's no better way to warm you through. They also work out as a very inexpensive way of feeding the family – a soup for six can easily cost less than a pound.

If you're using a starter to serve before a main meal, make sure you balance the two. So, if you're having mushrooms in red wine to begin with, you don't want the second course to be mushroom risotto!

miniature meatballs

400 g (14 oz) lean beef, minced
90 g (3 oz) fresh wholemeal breadcrumbs
1 tbsp chopped parsley
1 garlic clove, finely chopped
$1/8$ tsp salt
freshly ground black pepper
$1/2$ tbsp virgin olive oil

Spanish sauce:
1 tbsp virgin olive oil
1 onion
2 garlic cloves, chopped
1 sweet red pepper, chopped
250 g (8 oz) ripe tomatoes, skinned, seeded and chopped, or 200 g (7 oz) canned tomatoes, drained and chopped
$1/8$ tsp freshly ground black pepper
60 ml (2 fl oz) medium sherry

To make the sauce, heat the oil in a heavy casserole and fry the onion and garlic until they are soft but not browned. Add the chopped red pepper, tomatoes, salt and some black pepper, and simmer the mixture over a low heat for 20 minutes. While it cooks, prepare the meatballs.

Preheat the oven to 180°C (350°F or Mark 4). Combine the beef, breadcrumbs, parsley, garlic, egg and 2 tablespoons of water in a large mixing bowl. Add the salt and some black pepper and mix the ingredients until they are thoroughly blended. With dampened hands, shape the mixture into 36 miniature meatballs, each slightly smaller than a walnut.

Heat the oil in a heavy frying pan and fry the meatballs, shaking the pan and turning constantly to prevent them from sticking, until they are browned all over. Remove the meatballs from the pan with a slotted spoon and drain them on paper towels. Transfer the sauce to a blender or food processor, add the sherry, and puree the mixture. Return the sauce to the casserole, add the drained meatballs, and bake them for 40 minutes in the oven. Serve hot.

serves 6
working time 40 mins
total time 1 hour 30 mins

calories 220
total fat 8 g
saturated fat 2 g

hints and tips

As an alternative to beef why not try minced lamb, pork, turkey or chicken.

Ultimate
budget cookbook

mediterranean vegetable stew

2 large tomatoes, skinned, seeded and chopped
6 baby artichokes (350 g/12 oz), trimmed and halved
2 tbsp fresh lemon juice
4 celery sticks, sliced
1 fennel bulb, thinly sliced
3 thin leeks, trimmed and sliced into 1 cm (^{1}/$_2$ inch) rings
1 tbsp virgin olive oil
300 g (10 oz) chestnut or button mushrooms, stalks trimmed, cut in half
^{1}/$_2$ tsp salt
freshly ground black pepper
1 tbsp chopped fennel leaves

In a large, heavy saucepan, heat the tomatoes, artichokes and lemon juice, stirring frequently until the mixture comes to the boil. Continue to cook the vegetables over a high heat, stirring occasionally, for another 10 minutes.

Add the celery, fennel, leeks and bay leaf to the tomatoes and artichokes and simmer uncovered, stirring occasionally, until the vegetables are almost tender – about 20 minutes.

Meanwhile, in a small, heavy-bottomed saucepan, sauté the onions in the oil until they are soft and well browned – about 20 minutes. Shake the saucepan frequently to prevent the onions from sticking to the bottom or burning.

When the vegetables in the large pan are nearly cooked, add the mushrooms and simmer for another 10 minutes. Remove the pan from the heat and mix in the salt, some pepper and the onions. Leave the mixture to cool for about 2 hours.

Remove the bay leaf and discard it. Before serving, transfer the stew to a large serving dish and sprinkle the fennel leaves over the top.

serves 6
working time 35 mins
total time 2 hours 45 mins
(includes cooling)

calories 45
total fat 3 g saturated fat 1 g

mushroom risotto

60 g (2 oz) dried mushrooms
45 g (1½ oz) unsalted butter
1 onion, finely chopped
1 litre (1¾ pints) unsalted chicken stock
400 g (14 oz) brown rice
4 tbsp white wine
45 g (1½ oz) grated Parmesan cheese
2 tbsp chopped parsley
freshly ground black pepper

Soak the dried mushrooms in warm water for 5 minutes to remove grit. Drain them in a colander and soak them again in 600 ml (1 pint) of warm water until they are soft – 10 to 15 minutes. Strain off and reserve their second soaking liquid.

In a large saucepan, heat 30 g (1 oz) of the butter and sauté the onion until it is transparent – 3 to 5 minutes. Meanwhile, bring the chicken stock to the boil in a second pan, add the soaking water from the mushrooms, and simmer the liquid over low heat.

Chop the mushrooms roughly and add them to the onions in the pan. Stir the rice into the onion and mushroom mixture and cook it over a gentle heat for about 5 minutes, stirring constantly, to ensure the grains are well coated with the butter.

Pour the wine into the rice, then begin adding the hot stock, 2 or 3 ladlefuls at a time, stirring frequently. When one batch of liquid has almost been absorbed by the rice, add another few ladlefuls and continue to stir. Cook the rice until it is moist but not swimming in stock, and the grains are no longer brittle but still retain a chewy core – about 25 to 30 minutes.

Remove the rice from the heat and stir in the remaining butter, the Parmesan cheese, 1 tbsp of the parsley and some pepper. Cover the pan and leave the risotto to rest for 5 minutes before serving it in soup bowls, sprinkled with parsley.

serves 8
working time (and total time)
1 hour 20 mins

calories 285
total fat 8 g
saturated fat 4 g

hints and tips

As an alternative to brown rice try arborio rice which makes an excellent risotto.

ULTIMATE
budget cookbook

marinated sardines

600 g (1¼ lb) fresh sardines, scaled, heads and tails removed and gutted, rinsed and patted dry
2 garlic cloves
1 tbsp chopped parsley
1 tbsp virgin olive oil
125 ml (4 fl oz) wine vinegar

Remove the backbone from the sardines and separate the two fillets lengthwise, leaving the skin intact. Sprinkle the fish with the salt and place a layer of the fillets, skin side up, in a shallow, non-reactive dish. Top the sardines with the garlic and parsley. If the dish is not large enough to accommodate all the sardines in a single layer, add a second layer on top of the first.

Pour the oil and the vinegar over the fish, until the mixture covers the sardines. Cover the dish with plastic film and place it in the refrigerator to marinate for two to three days before serving.

serves 6
working time 45 mins
total time 2–3 days
(inc marinating)

calories 110
total fat 8 g saturated fat 2 g

hints and tips

Fresh sardines are now readily available in supermarkets as well as fishmongers.

mint-stuffed courgettes
with tomato coulis

6 small courgettes, halved lengthwise
45 g (1¹/2 oz) fresh mint leaves
125 g (4 oz) low-fat curd cheese
2 tbsp breadcrumbs
¹/4 tsp salt
Freshly ground black pepper
2 egg whites

tomato coulis:
500 g (1 lb) fresh tomatoes, skinned seeded and chopped, or 400 g (14 oz) canned plum tomatoes
1 garlic clove
1 tsp chilli powder
15 g (¹/2 oz) unsalted butter
¹/4 tsp salt

Cook the courgettes in salted boiling water until they are just tender – about 5 minutes. Drain them in a colander, rinse them in cold water, and leave them to cool on paper towels.

Preheat the oven to 200°C (400°F or Mark 6). When the courgettes are cool enough to handle, scoop out their centers with a teaspoon and transfer the flesh to a blender. Add the mint leaves and purée the mixture. Place the purée in a large bowl and add the curd cheese, breadcrumbs, salt and plenty of black pepper. In another bowl, beat the egg whites until they are stiff, fold them into the stuffing.

Arrange the hollowed out courgettes on a greased baking sheet and fill the centres with the stuffing. Bake in the oven for about 25 minutes, until the stuffing acquires a golden tinge.

Meanwhile bring the tomatoes to the boil in a saucepan. Add the garlic and the chilli powder and simmer the mixture for 15 minutes. Put the tomatoes into the blender with the butter and salt, and blend until the tomatoes break down to a purée and the butter is mixed in. if you are using canned tomatoes, pass the sauce through a sieve. Return the sauce to the pan and cook over gentle heat until it is heated through – 5 minutes. Serve the courgettes hot, accompanied by the tomato coulis.

serves 6
working time 30 mins
total time 50 mins

calories 55
total fat 2 g
saturated fat 1 g

hints and tips

As an alternative to curd cheese why not try cottage cheese.

ULTIMATE
budget cookbook

herbed vegetable brochettes

2 small courgettes, trimmed and cut into 1 cm ($^1/_3$ inch) rounds

12 small button mushrooms

12 baby sweet corn cobs, cut into 2 or 3 pieces

$^1/_2$ sweet pepper, cut into 12 squares

12 cherry tomatoes

6 lime wedges for garnish

herb marinade:

4 tbsp virgin olive oil

2 tbsp fresh lemon juice

$^1/_2$ tsp grated lemon rind

1 garlic clove

1 tsp Dijon mustard

3 tbsp chopped mixed herbs, such as basil marjoram and thyme

In a bowl, whisk together all the marinade ingredients to blend them well. Add the vegetables to the marinade, turning them to coat them evenly. Cover the bowl with plastic film and set aside for at least 6 hours, stirring the vegetables occasionally.

Twenty minutes before you plan to cook the brochettes, soak 12 bamboo skewers in water – this prevents them burning under the grill.

Preheat the grill. With a slotted spoon, remove the vegetables from the bowl, reserving the marinade. Thread a selection of vegetables on to each skewer. Grill the brochettes, about 10 cm (4 inches) from the heat source, turning them occasionally until the vegetables begin to brown – about 10 minutes. Serve the brochettes hot, with the reserved marinade spooned over them. Garnish with lime wedges.

serves 6
working time 25 mins
total time 6 hours 30 mins

calories 115
total fat 10 g
saturated fat 2 g

bacon-stuffed mushrooms

4 large field mushrooms
(about 300 g (10 oz)), rinsed, dried,
stalks removed
1 tbsp dry vermouth
4 tbsp coarsely chopped parsley
100 g (3^1/$_2$ oz) lean unsmoked
bacon rashers, trimmed of fat
1 garlic clove, crushed
1 tbsp virgin olive oil
15 g (^{1}/$_2$ oz) fresh wholemeal
breadcrumbs
freshly ground black pepper

Arrange the mushrooms, caps upside down, in a single layer in a shallow dish, and sprinkle with the dry vermouth and parsley. Cover the mushroom caps loosely with plastic film. To make the stuffing, cut the bacon into strips. Put the bacon and the crushed garlic in a bowl, stir in the olive oil, and microwave on high until the bacon begins to release its juices — about 1 minute. Cover the stuffing with plastic film and keep it warm while you cook the mushrooms.

Leaving the mushrooms loosely covered, microwave on high for 3 minutes, until they are just tender. Remove the plastic film, spread the bacon stuffing on top of the mushroom caps and microwave on high until they are hot — 30 seconds. Serve immediately.

serves 2
working (and total) time
20 mins

calories 100
total fat 6 g
saturated fat 2 g

28

spirals with lemon juice and dill

250 g (8 oz) pasta spirals
$1/4$ litre (8 fl oz) milk
$1/2$ tsp salt
4 tbsp vodka
1 tsp caraway seeds
3 tbsp fresh lemon juice
5 cm (2 inches) strip of lemon rind
2 tbsp fresh dill
or 2 tsp dried dill

Put the milk, salt, vodka, caraway seeds, lemon juice and lemon rind in a large nonstick pan. Bring to the boil, reduce the heat and simmer gently for 3 minutes. Add the spirals and enough water to almost cover them. Cover the pan and cook over a low heat, removing the lid and stirring occasionally, until the spirals are al dente and about 4 tablespoons of sauce remains – approximately 15 minutes. If necessary, add more water to keep the spirals from sticking. Remove the lemon rind and discard it. Stir in the chopped dill and serve immediately.

serves 4
working (and total) time
20 mins

calories 290
total fat 3 g
saturated fat 1 g

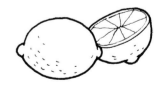

tossed salad with eggs and French beans

1/2 small red onion, cut thinly into rings

1 small red lollo lettuce, leaves torn

30 g (1 oz) rocket, washed and dried

90 g (3 oz) French beans, topped and blanched for 3 mins in boiling water

2 hard-boiled eggs, each cut into 6 wedges

6 black olives

3 red basil sprigs

3 green basil sprigs

vinaigrette dressing:
1 garlic clove, crushed
1/4 tsp salt
1 tbsp red wine vinegar
3tb virgin olive oil

First, prepare the vinaigrette. Place the garlic, salt and some pepper into a large salad bowl. Using a wooden pestle, pound the ingredients until they break down into a paste. Add the vinegar and stir until the salt dissolves. Pour in the olive oil and mix well.

With your hands, stir the onion slices into the vinaigrette and coat them well. Set them aside to marinate for 30 minutes.

Cross a pair of salad servers over the bottom of the bowl, to keep the dressing separate from the leaves that will be added before the salad is tossed. Lay a few of the largest lettuce leaves on the servers, then fill the bowl with the remaining lettuce and the rocket.

Top the leaves with the French beans, egg wedges, olives and basil. Draw out the servers from the bed of lettuce and rocket and toss the salad with the servers until all its ingredients are lightly coated with the dressing.

serves 6
working time 15 mins
total time 40 mins (inc marinating)

calories 115
total fat 10 g
saturated fat 2 g

hints and tips

Feel free to substitute the lollo lettuce and rocket with other types of salad leaves.

steamed cucumber with herb and yoghurt sauce

1 large cucumber
freshly ground black pepper
250 g (8 oz) thick Greek yoghurt
1 tbsp chopped fresh dill
1 tbsp chopped parsley
$1/2$ tbsp chopped fresh tarragon
4 fresh tarragon sprigs

With a sharp knife, peel the cucumber and chop it into 2.5 cm (1 inch) pieces. Remove the seeds from the centre of each piece with an apple corer. Pour enough water into a pan to fill it about 2.5 cm (1 inch) deep. Set a vegetable steamer in the pan and bring the water to the boil. Place the cucumber pieces in the steamer, season with some black pepper, cover the saucepan and steam until the cucumber is just heated through – 3 to 4 minutes.

While the cucumber is steaming, prepare the sauce by mixing together the Greek yoghurt, dill, parsley and chopped tarragon in a small pan. Heat over a very low heat until the yoghurt is warm, but not hot – about 1 minute.

Using a slotted spoon, transfer the cucumber pieces to warmed plates. Garnish the cucumber with the tarragon sprigs and serve with the warm yoghurt sauce.

serves 4
working and total time 20 mins

calories 50
total fat 3 g
saturated fat 2 g

creamed mushrooms on toast

2 slices granary bread
150 ml (^{1}/$_4$ pint) unsalted chicken
stock
1 tbsp Madeira
1 tsp fresh lemon juice
175 g (6 oz) button mushrooms,
wiped clean
2 tbsp crème fraîche
^{1}/$_4$ tsp salt
freshly ground black pepper
^{1}/$_2$ tsp Dijon mustard
^{1}/$_2$ sp mustard seeds

Toast the slices of bread on one side only and set aside.

Pour the stock, Madeira and lemon juice into a shallow, lidded saucepan and bring to the boil. Reduce the heat, add the mushrooms and simmer for about 4 minutes. Remove the mushrooms and set aside.

To reduce the cooking liquid, place the saucepan over high heat and boil until about 2 tablespoons of liquid remain. Add the crème fraîche and reduce further for a few seconds. Return the mushrooms to the liquid, warm through, and season with the salt, some pepper and the mustard.

Pour the mixture on to the untoasted side of the bread, sprinkle with the mustard seeds and place under a hot grill for about 20 seconds, until the seeds pop. Serve at once.

serves 2
working and total time 15 mins

calories 150
total fat 5 g
saturated fat 2 g

cheese and bacon granary bars

45 g (1^1/$_2$ oz) rindless bacon, minced
150 g (5 oz) granary flour
150 g (5 oz) plain flour
3 tsp baking flour
^{1}/$_8$ tsp salt
45 g (1^1/$_2$ oz) unsalted butter
45 g (5 oz) grated cheddar cheese
1 tbsp chopped fresh oregano
1 tbsp fresh lemon juice
15 ml (^{1}/$_4$ pint) skimmed milk
150 g (5 oz) low-fat fromage frais or mayonnaise
^{1}/$_4$ crisp lettuce, sliced
^{1}/$_4$ cucumber, thinly sliced
6 spring onions, sliced

Preheat the oven to 230°C (450°F or Mark 8), and grease and flour a baking sheet.

Dry fry the bacon until lightly browned. Cool on paper towels.

Sift the granary flour with the plain flour, baking powder and salt. Rub in the butter until the mixture resembles fine breadcrumbs. Stir in the bacon and cheese and the oregano. Add the lemon juice to the milk then less gradually mix sufficient liquid into the dry ingredients to make soft, but not sticky dough.

Transfer the dough to a floured work surface and shape it into a rectangle measuring about 25 by 10 cm (10 by 4 inches). Lift the dough onto the prepared baking sheet. Mark the top of the dough into six bars, cutting into the dough. Bake until well risen, firm to the touch and golden – about 20 minutes. Cool on a wire rack.

Cut each bread into six marked bars and split each one in half. Fill the bars with the fromage frais or mayonnaise and the lettuce, cucumber and spring onion slices.

serves 6
working time 30 mins
total time 1 hour 30 mins

calories 315
total fat 10 g
saturated fat 6 g

cream of chicken soup

1.5 kg (3 lb) chicken
1.5 l (2^1/$_2$ pints) unsalted vegetable stock
1 bay leaf
2 blades of mace
1 small bunch of parsley
15 g (^{1}/$_2$ oz) softened butter
15 g (^{1}/$_2$ oz) flour
3 tbsp double cream
freshly ground black pepper
chopped parsley for garnish

Wipe the chicken well and place in a large pan with the stock, bay leaf, mace, parsley and salt. Bring to the boil over medium heat, skim the scum from the surface, then reduce the heat to low. Cover the pan and cook the chicken gently for 1 hour.

Strain the stock through a sieve into a large jug. Cool the stock rapidly by standing the jug in very cold water for about 30 minutes. When the fat has congealed, remove it from the surface of the cooled stock.

Meanwhile, remove and discard the skin and bones from the chicken. Cut the flesh into small pieces.

Put the chicken pieces and cooled stock into a blender and purée until very smooth. Return the soup to the pan.

Blend the butter and flour together to make a smooth paste. Heat the soup almost to the boil, then gradually whisk in the butter and flour. Bring to the boil, stirring all the time, then reduce the heat and simmer the soup for 10 minutes. Stir in the cream and season with pepper. Serve garnished with parsley.

serves 6
working time 20 mins
total time 2 hours

calories 240
total fat 10 g
saturated fat 5 g

ULTIMATE
budget cookbook

lamb broth with winter vegetables

1 tbsp safflower oil

1 small onion, thinly sliced and separated into rings

750 g (1^1/$_2$ lb) lamb shoulder, knuckle end trimmed

4 tbsp pearl barley

1 bay leaf

1 tsp chopped fresh thyme or ^{1}/$_4$ tsp dried thyme

1 garlic clove, finely chopped

^{1}/$_2$ tsp salt

^{1}/$_4$ tsp crushed black peppercorns

1 turnip, peeled and cut into 1 cm (^{1}/$_2$ inch) cubed

1 small swede, peeled and cut into 1 cm (^{1}/$_2$ inch) cubed

1 carrot

Heat the oil in a large saucepan over medium heat. Add the onion rings and cook them until they are browned – about 8 minutes. Add the lamb, bay leaf, thyme, garlic, salt and peppercorns. Pour in 3 litres (5 ^{1}/$_4$ pints) of water and bring the liquid to the boil. Reduce the heat and simmer, partially covered, for 1^1/$_2$ hours.

Remove the bay leaf and discard it. Remove the lamb joint from the pan. When the lamb is cool enough to handle, slice the meat from the bone and cut into small cubes. Return the lamb cubes to the pan. Simmer the soup, uncovered, over medium heat until it is reduced by half – about 15 minutes. Add the turnip, swede and carrot and cover the pan. Simmer until the vegetables are tender – about 15 minutes more. Serve immediately.

serves 6
working time 15 mins
total time 2 hours

calories 205
total fat 14 g
saturated fat 7 g

turkey-lentil soup

750 g (1^1/$_2$ lb) turkey drumsticks, skinned
freshly ground black pepper
2 tsp safflower oil
1 small onion, thinly sliced
190 g (7 oz) lentils, picked over and rinsed
1 small bay leaf
1 small carrot, thinly sliced
1 small courgette, thinly sliced
1 stick celery, thinly sliced
1 ripe tomato, skinned, seeded and coarsely chopped
^{1}/$_2$ tsp finely chopped fresh sage or
^{1}/$_4$ tsp dried sage
^{3}/$_8$ tsp salt

Sprinkle the drumsticks with some pepper. Heat the oil in a large pan, over medium heat. Add the drumsticks and cook them, turning them frequently, until they are evenly browned – 2 to 3 minutes. Push the drumsticks to one side then add the onion and cook until it is translucent – 2 to 3 minutes.

Pour 1.25 litres (2 pints) of water into the pan. Add the lentils and bay leaf, and bring the water to the boil. Reduce the heat to maintain a simmer and cook the lentils, covered, for 20 minutes. Skim off any impurities that have risen to the surface. Continue cooking until the juices run clear from a drumstick pierced with the tip of a knife – about 20 minutes or more.

Remove the drumsticks and set them aside. When they are cool enough to handle, slice the meat from the bones and cut into small pieces. Discard the bones. Remove and discard the bay leaf. Add the carrot, courgette, celery and tomato to the soup and simmer until the vegetables are tender – about 5 minutes. Add the turkey, sage and salt and continue cooking the soup until the vegetables are tender – about 2 minutes more. Serve hot.

serves 6
working time 15 mins
total time 1 hour

calories 220
total fat 5 g
saturated fat 1 g

hints and tips

Chicken drumsticks can be used as an alternative to turkey.

ULTIMATE
budget cookbook

black-eyed bean and spring greens soup

190 g (7 oz) dried black-eyed beans

1 tbsp safflower oil

125 g (4 oz) chopped onion

30 g (1 oz) back bacon, cut into

5 mm ($^1/_4$ inch) dice)

1 garlic clove

1 bay leaf

$^1/_4$ tsp crushed hot red pepper flakes

1.25 litres (2 pints) unsalted chicken stock

250 g (8 oz) spring greens, trimmed and coarsely chopped

1 tsp salt

2 tsp cider vinegar

Rinse the beans under cold water, then put them into a large heavy pan and pour in enough cold water to cover them by about 7.5 cm (3 inches). Discard any beans that float to the surface. Cover the pan, leaving the lid ajar, and slowly bring the liquid to the boil over medium-low heat. Boil the beans for 2 minutes, then turn off the heat, cover the pan and let the beans soak for at least 1 hour.

Heat the oil in a large pan, over medium heat. Add the onion and sauté it, stirring occasionally, until it is translucent – about 4 minutes. Add the bacon and garlic and cook for 2 minutes, stirring frequently.

Drain the beans and add them to the pan, along with the bay leaf, red pepper flakes and stock. Bring the liquid to the boil, then reduce the heat to maintain a simmer, and partially cover the pan. Cook the mixture for 40 minutes, stirring gently several times. Toss in the spring greens and the salt, and cook until the greens are soft and the beans are tender – about 10 minutes. Remove and discard the bay leaf. Stir in the vinegar and serve immediately.

serves 6
working time 45 mins
total time 2 hours 30 mins
(inc soaking)

calories 130
total fat 5 g saturated fat 1 g

hints and tips

Why not try different types of beans in this dish. There are many varieties available, check your local shop or supermarket.

sweetcorn and coriander soup

10 g ($^{1}/_{3}$ oz) unsalted butter
1 tsp safflower oil
1 onion, finely chopped
3 garlic cloves, finely chopped
1 tsp ground cumin (optional)
1 sweet green pepper, seeded and chopped
1 sweet red pepper, seeded and chopped
1 green chilli pepper (optional), seeded and finely chopped
1 ripe tomato, skinned, seeded, chopped
350 g (12 oz) frozen or canned sweetcorn kernels
$^{1}/_{2}$ litre (16 fl oz) chicken stock
$^{1}/_{2}$ tsp salt
2 tbsp chopped fresh coriander

Heat the butter and oil in a large pan, over medium heat. Add the onion, garlic and cumin. Cook, stirring often, until the onion is translucent – about 5 minutes.

Stir in all the peppers and cook them until they soften slightly – about 2 minutes more. Add the tomato, sweetcorn, stock and salt. Reduce heat and simmer for 5 minutes.

Stir in the coriander just before serving.

serves 4
working and total
time 20 mins

calories 160
total fat 5 g
saturated fat 2 g

onion soup

15 g ($^1/_2$ oz) unsalted butter
1 tbsp safflower oil
1 kg (2 lb) onions, finely sliced
2 garlic cloves, finely chopped
2 litres (3$^1/_2$ pints) chicken or veal stock
$^1/_2$ litre (16 fl oz) dry white wine
2 tsp fresh thyme or
$^1/_2$ tsp dried thyme
2 tsp fresh lemon juice
$^1/_2$ tsp salt
$^1/_8$ tsp cayenne pepper
freshly ground black pepper
1 tbsp chopped fresh parsley

Melt the butter and oil in a large pan, over a medium-low heat. Add the onions and garlic and partially cover the pan. Cook for 3 minutes, stirring once. Remove the lid and continue cooking, stirring frequently, until the onions are browned – 20 to 35 minutes. Pour in 1.5 litres (2$^1/_2$ pints) of the stock and the wine, then add the thyme. Bring to the boil, lower the heat and simmer until it is reduced by one third – about 30 minutes. With a slotted spoon, remove about 150 g (5 oz) of the onions and set them aside.

Purée the soup in a blender. Return the soup to the pan and stir in the reserved onions. Pour in the remaining stock, then add the lemon juice, salt, cayenne pepper and some black pepper. Reheat the soup over a medium heat for 2 minutes. Sprinkle the parsley over the soup just before serving.

serves 8
working time 45 mins
total time 1 hour 15 mins

calories 200
total fat 9 g
saturated fat 4 g

turnip soup

22 g ($^3/_4$ oz) unsalted butter

500 g (1 lb) small white turnips, peeled, quartered and thinly sliced crosswise

$^1/_4$ tsp salt

$^1/_4$ tsp grated nutmeg

$^3/_4$ litre (1$^1/_4$ pints) unsalted chicken stock

3 small waxy potatoes

2 tbsp loosely packed fresh chervil leaves or chopped fresh parsley

Melt the butter in a large, heavy saucepan over medium heat. Stir in the turnips and cook them, stirring frequently, until they are golden-brown – approximately 20 minutes.

Season the turnips with the salt and nutmeg, and toss gently. Remove and reserve 75 g (2$^1/_2$ oz) of the turnips to use as a garnish.

Pour the stock into the pan; then cover it and bring the liquid to the boil. Reduce the heat and simmer the soup for 20 minutes, skimming off any foam that rises to the surface.

At the end of the 20 minutes, peel and quarter the potatoes, then cut them crosswise into thin slices and add them to the soup. Simmer the soup until the potatoes are tender but still intact – 10 to 15 minutes. Taste the soup for seasoning and add more nutmeg if necessary. Garnish the soup with the chervil or parsley and the reserved turnips before serving.

serves 4
working time 45 mins
total time 1 hour

calories 130
total fat 6 g
saturated fat 3 g

hints and tips

You could use parsnips instead of turnips ... and stir in a teaspoon of honey at the end.

ULTIMATE
budget cookbook

bean soup

360 g (12 oz) dried haricot bans, picked over
1.5 litres (2¹/₂ pints) chicken stock
1 onion
1 carrot, halved crosswise
1 stick celery, halved crosswise
1 leek, trimmed, split and washed
1 bay leaf
2 tsp fresh thyme or ¹/₂ tsp dried thyme
1 whole garlic bulb, skin removed
1 tsp salt
1 tbsp virgin olive oil
3 ripe tomatoes, skinned, seeded and chopped
30 g (1 oz) fresh parsley, chopped plus 1 tbsp for garnish
freshly ground black pepper

Rinse the beans under cold water. Put into a large pan, cover with water by about 75 mm (3 inches). Discard any beans that float to the surface. Cover the pan, leaving the lid ajar, slowly bringing the liquid to the boil over medium-low heat. Boil the beans for 2 minutes then turn off the heat, then soak, covered, for at least one hour. Drain the beans and return them to the pan. Pour in the stock, add the onion, carrot, celery, leek, bay leaf and thyme. Slowly bring to the boil over medium-low heat. Simmer and cover the pan. Cook the beans, stirring occasionally and skimming off any foam, until they are tender – 1 to 1¹/₂ hours. Simmer the beans for 30 minutes. Add the garlic and the salt.

Near the end of cooking, pour the olive oil into a frying pan over high heat. Add the tomatoes and cook for 3 to 5 minutes, stirring frequently. Stir in 30 g (1 oz) of parsley and set the pan aside.

Drain the beans over a bowl. Discard the vegetables except the garlic. Return two thirds of the beans to the pan. Separate the garlic into cloves and skin. Purée the garlic and remaining beans with ¹/₄ litre (8 fl oz) of the reserved cooking liquid.

Transfer to the pan with the beans and stir in the remaining liquid. Reheat soup over low heat and fold in the tomato mixture. Cook for 1 to 2 minutes. Season and serve. Garnish with remaining parsley.

serves 6
working time 45 mins
total time 3 hours 20 min (including soaking)

calories 255
total fat 5 g
saturated fat 1 g

tomato soup

1 tbsp virgin olive oil
500 g (1 lb) onions, chopped
1 carrot, thinly sliced
1 tsp fresh thyme or $^1/_4$ tsp dried thyme
3 garlic cloves, chopped
freshly ground black pepper
800 g (1$^3/_4$ lb) canned tomatoes, seeded and coarsely chopped, with their juice
300 ml ($^1/_2$ pint) chicken or vegetable stock
$^1/_4$ tsp salt
60 g (2 oz) watercress sprigs, stems trimmed

Heat the oil in a large saucepan over medium heat. Add the onions, garlic and some pepper, and cook the mixture, stirring it often, until the onions are translucent — 7 to 10 minutes. Add the tomatoes and their juice, the stock and the salt. Reduce the heat and simmer for 30 minutes.

While the soup is cooking, purée the cheese and yoghurt together in a blender or food mill. Set the purée aside.

Now purée the soup in batches, processing each batch for about 1 minute. Return the puréed soup to the pan, bring it to a simmer over medium heat and add the watercress. Simmer the soup just long enough to wilt the watercress — about one minute — then ladle the soup into warmed serving bowls.

Serve the soup at once.

serves 6
working time 25 mins
total time 45 mins

calories 95
total fat 4 g
saturated fat 1 g

ULTIMATE
budget cookbook

curried yellow split pea soup

175 g (6 oz) dried yellow split peas,
rinsed
1 tbsp oil
350 g (12 oz) lamb shoulder,
knuckle end, trimmed of fat
1 onion, coarsely chopped
4 tbsp thinly sliced celery
2 tbsp curry powder
2 garlic cloves, finely chopped
1 small bay leaf
2 tbsp chopped fresh mint
1 carrot, thinly sliced
1 tsp salt
$1/4$ tsp white pepper
$1/2$ lemon, juice only
4 mint sprigs for garnish

In a large, heavy bottomed saucepan, heat the oil over medium-high heat and cook the lamb joint until it is brown all side – 3 to 5 minutes. Reduce the heat to medium and add the onion, celery and curry powder. Cook the vegetables, stirring constantly, until the onion turns translucent – 3 to 5 minutes. Add the garlic and continue to cook for 30 seconds, stirring to keep the mixture from burning. Add the peas, the bay leaf and 1.5 litres of water. Bring the mixture to the boil, skim off any impurities, then add the chopped mint. Partially cover the pan, reduce the heat, and simmer the soup until the meat and the peas are tender – about 1 hour.

Remove the lamb joint, and when it is cool enough to handle, trim the meat from the bone; cut the meat into bite-size pieces and set them aside. Remove the bay leaf from the peas and discard it. Purée the peas in a blender or food processor, then return them to the pan. Add the lamb and carrot, and cook, covered, over medium heat until the carrot slices are tender – about 5 minutes. Season the soup with the salt, some pepper and the lemon juice and serve.

serves 4
working time 30 mins
total time 2 hours 30 mins

calories 325
total fat 10 g
saturated fat 1 g

chicken gumbo

chicken with peanuts and ginger sauce

emerald chicken roll

cajun chicken wings

chicken in a tortilla pie

turkey crust pizza

greek style chicken and rice casserole

chicken braised with haricot beans and tomatoes

chicken thighs grilled with sherry and honey

jellied chicken with lemon and dill

chicken poached in milk and curry

braised chicken with potatoes, leeks and kale

chicken fricassee

chilled chicken couscous with orange

chicken stew with courgettes and tomatoes

chicken with orange and onion

yoghurt chicken drumsticks

Poultry generally is a great form of low-fat food. It's versatile and chicken, in particular, is inexpensive. You don't have to buy a whole chicken to get the best out of this high protein food as supermarkets sell portions. Duck contains the most fat of all the birds – and is generally one of the most expensive – but whatever you opt for be sure to discard the skin which has no nutritional value but contains an awful lot of fat and calories!

If you're buying fresh poultry (chicken, turkey or duck) make sure the bird is plump and has fresh-looking skin, with flesh that is white and firm.

If using frozen, make sure that the bird, or the joint, is thoroughly defrosted before you cook it. Look out for special supermarket promotions which can end up saving you money. As well as regularly offering a pound off poultry, many chains will do a two for one offer so it's worth taking advantage and sticking one pack in the freezer for another day.

chicken gumbo

1 tbsp finely chopped garlic

1 tbsp chopped fresh thyme or $^3/_4$ tsp dried thyme

1 tsp dry mustard

$^1/_2$ tsp salt

$^1/_2$ tsp paprika

$^1/_2$ tsp cracked black peppercorns

350 g (12 oz) chicken breast meat, cut crosswise into 1 cm ($^1/_2$ inch) wide strips

1 lemon (juice only)

15 g ($^1/_2$ oz) unsalted butter

1 large onion, sliced

5 sticks celery, cut lengthwise into 5 mm ($^1/_4$ inch) strips, each strip cut into $2^1/_2$ cm (1 inch) lengths

$1^1/_2$ tbsp flour

1.25 kg ($2^1/_2$ lb) ripe tomatoes, skinned, seeded and chopped or 800 g (28 oz) canned tomatoes, drained and chopped

2 bay leaves

1 tbsp olive oil

250 g (8 oz) okra, cut into $2^1/_2$ cm (1 inch) lengths

$^1/_2$ litre (16 fl oz) chicken stock

2 sweet peppers, one red, one green, seeded and cut lengthwise into 5 mm ($^1/_4$ inch) strips

Mix the garlic with the thyme, mustard, salt, paprika and pepper. Toss the chicken strips with one third of the mixture and the lemon juice. Set the chicken aside to marinate at room temperature.

Melt the butter in a large pan over medium-high heat. Add the onion and celery and sauté them, stirring frequently, until the onions are translucent – 8 minutes. Stir in the flour and the remaining spice mixture. Continue cooking for 2 minutes more. Add the tomatoes and bay leaves. Reduce the heat and simmer for 15 minutes.

Meanwhile, heat the olive oil in a frying pan over medium-high heat. Add the okra and sauté it, stirring frequently, until the pieces are browned – about 5 minutes. Set the okra aside.

Add the chicken strips, the stock and peppers to the tomato mixture. Simmer for 20 minutes more, stirring several times.

Before serving, stir the okra into the stew and allow it to heat through.

serves 6
working time 35 mins
total time 1 hour and 10 mins

calories 295
total fat 12 g
saturated fat 3 g

Hints and tips

Keep a tin or two of chopped tomatoes in your cupboard, they can be handy for dishes like this, as ripe tomatoes may not always be readily available.

ULTIMATE
budget cookbook

chicken with peanuts and ginger sauce

750 g (1½ lb) chicken breast meat, cut into 1 cm (½ inch) cubes
125 ml (4 fl oz) dry white wine
45 g (1½ oz) fresh ginger, finely chopped
1 garlic clove, crushed
¼ tsp salt
freshly ground black pepper
¼ litre (8 fl oz) chicken stock
2 tbsp peanut butter
1 tsp tomato purée
2 spring onions, julienned
45 g (1½ oz) peanuts, crushed with a rolling pin
1 tbsp safflower oil

Make a marinade of the wine, ginger, garlic, salt and pepper and let the chicken stand in it two hours. Near the end of the marinating time, prepare the sauce. Pour the stock into a small pan and whisk in the peanut butter and tomato purée.

Add the spring onions and simmer the sauce over a low heat, uncovered, for 2 minutes. Remove the pan from the heat and set aside.

Remove the cubes from the marinade and set them aside. Strain the marinade and add it to the sauce. Return the mixture to a simmer and cook over a low heat, stirring occasionally, until the sauce is thick enough to coat the back of a spoon – about 4 minutes. Remove the pan from the heat.

Roll the chicken cubes in the peanuts, sparsely coating the cubes. Heat the oil in a frying pan over a high heat. When the oil is hot, add the chicken cubes and lightly brown them, stirring gently to keep intact as much of the peanut coating as possible – about 3 minutes. Remove the pan from the heat and allow the chicken to finish cooking as it rests in the hot pan – about 2 minutes more. Transfer the chicken to a warmed platter and pour the sauce over it just before serving.

serves 6
working time 20 mins
total time 2 hours 20 mins

calories 260
total fat 12 g
saturated fat 3 g

emerald chicken roll

500 g (1 lb) chicken breast meat, cut into 5 cm (2 inch) pieces
7 g ($^1/_4$ oz) dried mushrooms
12–15 large Cos lettuce leaves
1 tbsp chopped parsley
$^1/_2$ tsp chopped fresh tarragon leaves or $^1/_2$ tsp dried tarragon
2 spring onions, green stalks trimmed to 5 cm (2 inch) of the white part, cut into pieces
$^1/_2$ tsp ground coriander
$^1/_4$ tsp salt
freshly ground black pepper
250 g (8 oz) low-fat ricotta cheese
1 egg white
$^1/_2$ tbsp cornflour, mixed with 2 tbsp Madeira or port
15 g ($^1/_2$ oz) unsalted butter
2 tbsp finely cut fresh chives

Put the mushrooms in a small bowl and pour 300 ml ($^1/_2$ pint) boiling water over them. Cover them and set aside for 30 minutes. Meanwhile, place the lettuce leaves in a large pot with a tight-fitting lid and pour 125 ml (4 fl oz) of cold water over them. Place a piece of tinfoil on top of the lettuce and cover. Bring the water to the boil and steam the leaves for 1 minute to make them limp. Remove the pan from the heat and take off the lid and foil. When the leaves are cool enough to handle, cut out the thick core at the base of each stem. Spread the leaves on paper towels to drain.

Put the chicken in the bowl of a food processor. Add the chopped parsley, tarragon, spring onion, coriander, salt and lots of pepper. Process in short bursts, until the chicken is coarsely chopped. Add the ricotta cheese and the chicken stock and purée until smooth. Scrape down the sides of the bowl, then, with the motor running, add the egg white and process it until it is thoroughly mixed – about 5 seconds more.

Remove the mushrooms from the water and squeeze them over the bowl to rid them of excess water. Strain and reserve the soaking liquid. Chop the mushrooms into coarse pieces and add them to the processor bowl. Using a few short bursts, process just enough to incorporate the mushrooms into the chicken mixture. Poach a spoonful of the mixture in simmering water. Taste and correct the seasonings if necessary.

serves 8
working time 45 mins
total time 1 hour and 15 mins

calories 145
total fat 6 g
saturated fat 3 g

Spread a piece of muslin – about 45 cm (18 inches) long – on a work surface. Lay the lettuce leave in a row, each long edge overlapping the next to form a rectangle roughly 40x20 cm (16x8 inches). Spoon the chicken mixture in a row lengthwise down the centre of the rectangle. Use a rubber spatula dipped in cold water to shape the mixture into a log. Pull up the leaves on each side to cover the chicken, then roll the log in the muslin, tucking the ends of the muslin underneath, or tying them with string.

Add enough water to the mushroom-soaking liquid to total 350 ml (12 fl oz). Pour the liquid into a wok or other large pot, fitted with a rack or steamer. Place the chicken roll on the rack. Cover and steam the roll until it feels firm to the touch – about 25 minutes. Lift the roll out of the steamer and set aside. Remove the rack.

Stir the cornflour mixture into the liquid. Cook until the sauce is translucent and thick – about 1 minute. Remove the pot from the heat, add the butter and swirl the sauce until the butter melts. Stir the chives into the sauce.

Unwrap the chicken roll, letting any juices run into the sauce. Cut the roll into diagonal slices – about 2 cm ($3/4$ inch) thick, and arrange them on a serving platter. Pour the sauce into a heated sauceboat and serve it separately.

cajun chicken wings

12 chicken wings
5 dried bay leaves, crumbled
$^3/_4$ tbsp caraway seeds
$^1/_2$–$^3/_4$ tsp cayenne pepper
$^3/_4$ tsp ground coriander
$^3/_4$ tsp ground cumin
4 garlic cloves, finely chopped
1$^1/_2$ tsp dried mustard
2 tsp paprika
$^3/_4$ tsp dried thyme
$^1/_2$ tsp salt
2 tbsp brandy
2 tbsp fresh lemon or lime juice

De-fat the chicken wings by cooking in boiling water for 10 minutes. Drain and set aside to cool. Preheat the oven to 190°C (375°F or Mark 5).

Using a large mortar and pestle, grind the bay leaves to fine powder then add the caraway seeds, cayenne pepper, coriander, cumin, garlic, mustard, paprika, thyme, and salt and grind for about 10 minutes. Add the brandy and lemon or lime juice to the herbs and stir into a thick paste.

With a pastry brush, cover both sides of each wing with the herb paste. When no more paste remains, squeeze the last few drops from the brush. Arrange the chicken on a baking sheet.

Bake until the skin is deep brown and quite crisp – 30 to 35 minutes.

serves 4
working time 20 mins
total time 1 hour

calories 335
total fat 21 g
saturated fat 6 g

hints and tips

If you do not have any brandy then you can use sherry or even whisky as an alternative.

chicken in a tortilla pie

1.5 kg (3 lb) chicken, wings removed,
the rest skinned and quartered
125ml (4 fl oz) chicken stock
$1/4$ tsp ground coriander seeds
$1/8$ tsp cayenne pepper
$1/4$ tsp ground cumin
1 green pepper, finely chopped
4 spring onions, finely chopped
$1/4$ tsp dried oregano
1 tbsp virgin olive oil
freshly ground black pepper
175 g (6 oz) cheddar cheese, grated
225 cm (10 inch) flour tortillas
$1/8$ tsp chilli powder

salsa:
2 ripe tomatoes, chopped
1 or 2 green chilli peppers, chopped
2 garlic cloves, finely chopped
1 lime, juice only
1 tbsp chopped coriander or parsley
$1/4$ tsp salt
freshly ground black pepper

serves 4
working time 20 mins
total time 30 mins

calories 550
total fat 29 g
saturated fat 12 g

Place the chicken in a baking dish, with the meatier part of each piece towards the edge. Pour in the stock and sprinkle with coriander, cayenne pepper, and $1/8$ tsp of the cumin. Cover with greaseproof paper and microwave on high for 10 minutes.

Remove the breasts and microwave the legs for 2 minutes more. Let the meat stand until it is cool.

Discard the liquid and shred the meat.

Combine the green pepper, spring onions, oregano, oil, black pepper, and the remaining cumin in a bowl. Cover with plastic film. Cook for 2 minutes on high then remove from the oven and mix in the chicken.

In a separate bowl, mix the salsa ingredients. Add 125 ml (4 fl oz) of the salsa and half the cheese to the chicken. Place a tortilla on a plate, cover it with the chicken and put the other tortilla on top. Sprinkle with the remaining cheese and chilli powder. Microwave until the cheese melts. Cut into wedges and serve.

turkey crust pizza

1 kg (2 lb) white and dark turkey meat, finely chopped
45 g (1^1/$_2$ oz) dry breadcrumbs
1 chopped spring onion
2 lightly beaten egg whites
4 drops Tabasco
2 tsp virgin olive oil
^{1}/$_4$ tsp salt
freshly ground black pepper
2 tbsp white wine
150 g (5 oz) grated mozzarella and Gruyere cheese

pizza sauce:
1 tbsp virgin olive oil
90 g (3 oz) onion, finely chopped
1 green pepper, cut into strips
135 g (4^1/$_2$ oz) thinly sliced mushrooms
1 kg (35 oz) canned plum tomatoes
2 garlic cloves, finely chopped
2 tbsp red wine vinegar
2 tsp sugar

1 tbsp chopped fresh basil
^{1}/$_2$ tsp dried oregano
^{1}/$_4$ tsp salt
freshly ground black pepper

Place the oil in a pan, over medium-low heat and cook the onion for 3 minutes. Add the peppers and mushrooms and cook for 2 minutes. Add the rest of the sauce ingredients. Bring to the boil, reduce the heat and simmer for 40 minutes.

Preheat the oven to 200°C (400°F or Mark 6). Combine the breadcrumbs, spring onion, egg whites, Tabasco, 1 tsp of the oil and the salt and pepper in a large bowl. Add 125 ml (4 fl oz) of the sauce and the white wine. Mix in the turkey. Rub a shallow 25–30 cm (10–12 inch) round baking dish with the remaining oil. Spread the turkey mixture over the bottom of the dish, pushing it all around the sides, to resemble a crust. Pour half of the sauce onto the turkey crust, cover with the grated cheeses, ladle on the remaining sauce, sprinkle with freshly ground black pepper, bake for 15 minutes. Let stand for 5 minutes before serving.

serves 8
working time 30 mins
total time 1 hour 30 mins

calories 290
total fat 11 g
saturated fat 4 g

ULTIMATE
budget cookbook

greek style chicken and rice casserole

2 tbsp vegetable oil
8 chicken thighs, skinned
175 g (6 oz) long grain rice
1 onion, chopped
4 garlic cloves, finely chopped
$^1/_4$ litre (8 fl oz) chicken stock
800 g (28 oz) canned whole tomatoes
3 tbsp chopped fresh oregano
1 tbsp fresh thyme
12 oil-cured olives, stoned and quartered or 12 stoned black olives, chopped
30 g (1 oz) feta cheese, crumbled

Heat the oil in a large casserole over a medium-high heat. Add four of the thighs and cook until they are lightly browned – about 4 minutes each side. Remove the first four thighs and brown the other four. Set all the thighs aside.

Reduce the heat to medium, and add rice, onion, garlic, and 4 tbsp of the stock. Cook the mixture, stirring constantly, until the onion is translucent – about 4 minutes. Add the remaining stock, the tomatoes, oregano and thyme. Push the thighs down into the rice mixture. Bring to the boil, reduce the heat and simmer the chicken, tightly covered, until the rice is tender – 20 to 30 minutes.

Stir the olives into the chicken and rice and serve with the feta on top.

serves 8
total time 1 hour

calories 275
total fat 11 g
saturated fat 3 g

chicken braised with haricot beans and tomatoes

1.75 kg (3¹/₂ lb) skinless chicken
pieces
500 g (1 lb) dried haricot beans,
soaked overnight in water, and
drained
¹/₄ tsp salt
freshly ground black pepper
1 tbsp fresh thyme or ³/₄ tsp dried
thyme
2 tbsp safflower oil
125 ml (4 fl oz) dry white wine
2 leeks trimmed, sliced thinly
400 g (14 oz) canned peeled
tomatoes, halved, in their liquid
1 tbsp fresh rosemary or
³/₄ tbsp dried
6 garlic cloves, finely chopped
3 bay leaves
600 ml (1 pint) chicken stock
90 g (3 oz) dry breadcrumbs
2 tbsp virgin olive oil
2 tsp fresh chopped parsley

Place the beans in a pan and cover with 5 cm (2 inch) of water. Bring to the boil. Boil for 10 minutes, skimming off the foam. Reduce the heat. Stir in the pepper and one third of the thyme. Cover and simmer for 35 minutes and then drain. Preheat the oven to 195°C (375°F or Mark 5).

In a frying pan, heat the safflower oil over a medium-high heat. Add the chicken and brown lightly. Transfer to a plate. Pour off any fat and reserve. Pour the wine into the pan and deglaze over medium-high heat.

When boiling, add the leeks, tomatoes, rosemary, remaining thyme, salt, and half of the garlic. Simmer, stirring until tender – about 10 minutes.

Spread the remaining garlic over the bottom of a casserole. Add half of the beans in an even layer, then the chicken, then the bay leaves. Spoon half of the vegetable mixture on top. Add the remaining beans then spoon the remaining vegetables over. Pour in 350 ml (12 fl oz) of the stock and sprinkle the breadcrumbs over. Dribble on the reserved fat and olive oil.

Bake for 45 minutes. Pour in the remaining stock around the edges, without soaking breadcrumbs. Bake for 30 minutes or until topping is crunchy and golden, and beans are tender.

Garnish with parsley and serve.

serves 6
working time 1 hour
total time 1 day

calories 505
total fat 19 g
saturated fat 4 g

hints and tips

Instead of dried thyme and rosemary feel free to try a mixture, for example, dried Italian herbs.

chicken thighs grilled
with sherry and honey

8 skinned chicken thighs
1/4 litre (8 fl oz) dry sherry
3 tbsp honey
4 garlic cloves
3 tbsp red wine vinegar
1 tbsp soy sauce
1 tbsp cornflour, mixed with 2 tbsp
dry sherry
1/4 tsp salt

Boil the sherry in a small pan until it is reduced by half – about 7 minutes. Remove the pan from the heat and whisk in the honey, garlic, vinegar and soy sauce. Return the pan to the heat and whisk the cornflour mixture into the sauce. Bring to the boil and cook for 1 minute, whisking constantly. Remove the pan from the heat and let the sauce cool.

Preheat the grill. Sprinkle the salt on both sides of the thighs and lay them, bone up, on a rack in a roasting pan. Brush liberally with the sauce, then grill them 10 to 15 cm (4 to 6 inches) from the heat source for 6 to 7 minutes. Turn over and brush again with sauce. Grill for 3 or 4 minutes more, then brush again with the remaining sauce. Continue grilling until the juices run clear when a thigh is pierced with the tip of a sharp knife – 5 to 7 minutes more. Transfer the thighs to a platter and trickle any remaining sauce from the roasting pan over them.

serves 4
total time 25 mins

calories 340
total fat 11 g
saturated fat 3 g

jellied chicken with lemon and dill

Two 1.5 kg (3 lb) chickens, skinned
and cut into serving pieces.
$^1/_2$ tsp salt
freshly ground black pepper
2 tbsp virgin olive oil
1 large onion, finely chopped
5 tbsp chopped fresh dill
1 litre (1$^3/_4$ pints) chicken stock
3 large carrots, thinly sliced
125 g (4 oz) shelled peas
80 ml (3 fl oz) fresh lemon juice

Sprinkle the chicken pieces with the salt and pepper. Heat the olive oil in a frying pan and sauté the chicken pieces over medium-high heat until golden – about 5 minutes on each side. Arrange the pieces in a large casserole.

In the remaining oil, cook the onion over medium-low heat until translucent – about 10 minutes. Stir in half the dill. Spoon the onion mixture onto the chicken pieces. Pour the stock over all and bring to a simmer on top of the stove. After 20 minutes, turn the pieces, add the carrots and peas and continue cooking until the juices run clear when the chicken is pierced with the tip of a sharp knife – about 10 minutes more.

Pour the lemon juice over the chicken and vegetables and cool to room temperature. Sprinkle the remaining dill on top. Refrigerate for 6 hours or overnight to allow the natural gelatine to set. Serve cold.

serves 8
working time 30 mins
total time 1 day

calories 340
total fat 14 g
saturated fat 3 g

ULTIMATE
budget cookbook

chicken poached in milk and curry

1.5 kg (3 lb) chicken, wings reserved, the rest cut into serving pieces
$^3/_4$ litre (1$^1/_4$ pints) milk
2 large onions, thinly sliced
4 to 5 bay leaves
2 tsp fresh thyme or $^1/_2$ tsp dried thyme
3 garlic cloves, crushed
1 tsp curry powder
$^1/_2$ tsp salt
150 g (5 oz) shelled peas
15 g ($^1/_2$ oz) unsalted butter

In a pan, over a medium heat, mix the milk, onions, bay leaves, thyme, garlic, curry powder, salt and pepper. Bring to a simmer, then remove from heat. Allow to stand for 30 minutes. After 15 minutes, preheat the oven to 175°C (325°F or Mark3).

Arrange the chicken in a baking dish. Bring the milk mixture to a simmer again and pour it over the chicken. Set the saucepan aside, but do not wash it. drape the onions over any chicken pieces that protrude from the liquid, so the chicken will not dry out during cooking. Put the dish in the oven and poach the chicken until the juices run clear when a thigh is pierced with the tip of a sharp knife — 35 to 40 minutes.

Take the dish from the oven and turn the oven off. Remove the chicken pieces from the liquid and distribute them among four shallow serving bowls. Strain the poaching liquid into the pan, and use some onion slices to garnish. Discard the remaining onions. Keep the bowls warm in the oven.

Cook the liquid in the pan over medium heat until it is reduced by a quarter. Add the peas and cook them until tender — about 5 minutes. Remove the pan from the heat and whisk in the butter. Pour some of the sauce and peas over the chicken in each bowl and serve immediately.

serves 4
working time 15 mins
total time 1 hour 15 mins

calories 450
total fat 20 g
saturated fat 10 g

braised chicken with potatoes, leeks and kale

1.75 kg (3^1/$_2$ lb) chicken
freshly ground black pepper
^{3}/$_4$ tsp salt
1 tbsp safflower oil
1 leek, halved lengthwise and cut
into 1 cm (^{1}/$_2$ inch) slices
2 tbsp thinly sliced shallots
125 g (4 oz) fresh kale, stemmed
and coarsely chopped
2 tsp fresh thyme or ^{1}/$_2$ tsp dried
thyme
^{1}/$_2$ tsp cayenne pepper
3 red potatoes, unpeeled, cut into
4 cm (1^1/$_2$ inch) pieces.

Rub the inside of the chicken with pepper and ^{1}/$_4$ tsp of the salt, and truss the bird.

In a large casserole, heat the oil over medium-high heat. Add the leek, shallots and kale and sauté until the kale begins to wilt. Pour in 1 litre (1^3/$_4$ pints) of water, then add the remaining salt, some more pepper and the thyme. Place the chicken in the casserole and sprinkle the cayenne pepper over it. bring to the boil, reduce the heat to low, partially cover and simmer for 50 minutes.

Transfer the chicken from the casserole to a warmed platter. Cover it with foil to keep it warm. Skim off any fat in the casserole. Add the potatoes and simmer until they are tender – about 10 minutes. Arrange the vegetables round the chicken and pour the braising liquid over it.

serves 4
working time 30 mins
total time 1 hour 15 mins

calories 440
total fat 23 g
saturated fat 6 g

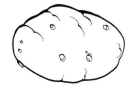

ULTIMATE
budget cookbook

chicken fricassee

4 large chicken thighs, meat cut into
2.5 cm (1 inch) cubes.
125 ml (4 fl oz) plain low-fat yoghurt
2 tbsp single cream
2 tbsp cornflour, mixed with
4 tbsp water
2 tsp fresh thyme or $^1/_2$ tsp
dried thyme
1 tsp fresh rosemary or $^1/_2$ tsp
dried rosemary
15 g ($^1/_2$ oz) butter
2 carrots, julienned
250 g (8 oz) mushrooms, thickly
sliced
3 tbsp finely chopped shallots
$^1/_2$ tsp ground cumin
125 ml (4 fl oz) dry white wine
125 ml (4 fl oz) chicken stock
4 garlic cloves, finely chopped
$^1/_4$ tsp salt

serves 4
working time 45 mins
total time 45 mins

calories 250
total fat 10 g
saturated fat 4 g

In a bowl, combine the yoghurt, cream, cornflour, thyme, and rosemary. Set aside.

Melt the butter in a frying pan. Add the carrots and cook for 2 minutes, stirring once. Stir in the chicken, mushrooms, shallots, wine, stock, garlic, salt and the yoghurt mixture. Reduce the heat to medium-low, cover and cook for 5 minutes.

Uncover and stir well. Cover again and cook until the chicken is done – 5 minutes. Drain the contents in a colander, catching the sauce in a bowl. Put the contents of the colander on a platter and keep warm.

Return the sauce to the pan. Over medium heat, whisking occasionally to keep the sauce from burning, reduce it by approximately half. This should take 10 to 15 minutes. Return the chicken mixture to the pan, and stir to coat the chicken with the sauce. Serve at once.

chilled chicken couscous with orange

350 g (12 oz) chicken, cut into
2 cm ($^3/_4$ inch) pieces
2 tbsp finely chopped onion
4 tbsp safflower oil
175 g (6 oz) couscous
$^1/_4$ litre (8 fl oz) chicken stock
5 tbsp fresh orange juice
1 garlic clove
4 tsp fresh thyme or 1 tsp
dried thyme
$^1/_4$ tsp salt
freshly ground black pepper
6 spring onions, finely chopped
1 red pepper, seeded and chopped
into 1 cm ($^1/_2$ inch) squares
lettuce leaves

In a frying pan with a tight-fitting lid, sauté the onion in 1 tbsp of the oil, over a medium-high heat for about 2 minutes. Stir in the couscous, stock and $^1/_4$ litre (8 fl oz) of water and boil rapidly for about 2 minutes. Remove the pan from the heat and cover it. let it stand for 5 minutes. Remove the lid, fluff up the couscous with a fork, and transfer the mixture to a large mixing bowl. Put in the fridge to cool.

For the dressing, combine 4 tablespoons of orange juice, garlic, thyme, salt and some pepper. Add half the spring onions and set aside.

Add another tablespoon of oil to the pan and set it over a high heat. When the oil is hot, add the chicken pieces and sauté them, stirring frequently, until lightly browned – 4 to 5 minutes. Stir in the remaining orange juice and a generous grinding of pepper. Using a slotted spoon, transfer the pieces to a bowl. Refrigerate for at least 10 minutes.

Whisk the remaining 2 tbsp of oil into the dressing mixture. Remove the couscous and chicken from the fridge. Stir the dressing into the couscous. Finally, add the chicken, the remaining spring onions and the red pepper, and mix well. Serve each portion on a bed of lettuce.

serves 4
working time 30 mins
total time 40 mins

calories 435
total fat 18 g
saturated fat 3 g

chicken stew with courgettes and tomatoes

1.25 kg (2^1/$_2$ lb) tomatoes, skinned,
seeded and chopped, or
800 g (28 oz) canned tomatoes,
chopped, with their juice
350 ml (12 fl oz) chicken stock
1 tsp sugar
2 garlic cloves, finely chopped
1 tsp dried basil
^{1}/$_2$ tsp chilli powder
^{1}/$_2$ tsp salt
freshly ground black pepper
2 chicken breasts, skinned
90 g (3 oz) wide egg noodles
250 g (8 oz) courgettes, trimmed
and cut into thick rounds

Put the tomatoes, stock, sugar, garlic, basil, chilli powder, salt and some pepper into a large pan over medium heat. Bring the liquid to a simmer and cook for 10 minutes.

Add the chicken breast to the pan and poach them for 12 minutes. With a slotted spoon, remove the slightly undercooked breasts and set them aside.

Cook the needles in 1.5 litres (1^1/$_2$ pints) of boiling water with ^{3}/$_4$ tsp of salt for 3 minutes. Drain the noodles well, then add them to the stew along with the courgette rounds. When the chicken breasts are cool enough to handle, remove the meat from the bones. Cut the meat into 10 mm (^{1}/$_2$ inch) pieces and return to the pan. Continue cooking the stew until the courgettes are tender – about 5 minutes more.

serves 4
working time 35 mins
total time 1 hour

calories 325
total fat 6 g
saturated fat 1 g

chicken with orange and onion

2 1.5 kg (3 lb) chickens, wings
removed, quartered and skinned
2 tbsp flour
$1/2$ tsp salt
freshly ground black pepper
2 tbsp safflower oil
1 orange, rind only, julienned
3 onions, thinly sliced
2 tsp fresh thyme or $1/2$ tsp dried
thyme
300 ml ($1/2$ pint) fresh orange juice
2 tbsp fresh lemon juice
1 tbsp honey
175 ml (6 fl oz) dry white wine

Dust the chicken pieces with the flour. Sprinkle them with $1/4$ teaspoon of the salt and some of the pepper.

In a large, heavy frying pan, heat the oil over medium-high heat and sauté the chicken in several batches until golden-brown – about 5 minutes on each side. Transfer the pieces to a 23 by 33 cm (9 by 13 inch) baking dish and scatter the orange rind over them.

Preheat the oven to 180°C (350°F or Mark 4). Over medium-low heat, cook the onions in the oil in the pan, stirring occasionally, until they are translucent – about 10 minutes. Stir in the thyme and the remaining salt and spread the mixture over the chicken pieces.

Pour the orange and lemon juice, honey and wine into the pan. Bring the liquid to the boil and reduce it to about $1/4$ litre (8 fl oz). Pour the liquid over the chicken. Cook the pieces uncovered in the oven, basting once with the liquid until the juices run clear when a thigh is pierced with the tip of a sharp knife – about 35 minutes.

serves 8
working time 30 mins
total time 1 hour 15 mins

calories 370
total fat 14 g
saturated fat 3 g

ULTIMATE
budget cookbook

yoghurt chicken drumsticks

16 chicken drumsticks, skinned
$^1/_2$ tsp salt
1 lemon, grated rind and juice
3 tbsp paprika
$^1/_2$ tsp Tabasco sauce
15 ml ($^1/_2$ pint) plain low-fat yoghurt
freshly ground black pepper

Cut two deep, diagonal slits in opposite sides of each drumstick. In a small bowl, stir the salt and the grated lemon rind into the lemon juice, then rub the mixture over each drumstick and into the slits. Place the drumsticks on a wire rack set over a baking tray, and sieve 1 tablespoon of the paprika evenly over the upper side of the drumsticks.

In another bowl, mix together the Tabasco sauce, yoghurt and some black pepper. Using a brush, coat the paprika-sprinkled side of each drumstick with the yoghurt mixture. Turn the drumsticks over, sieve another tablespoon of paprika over them, and coat them with the remaining yoghurt mixture. Set the drumsticks aside for 3 hours, until the yogurt begins to dry.

Lightly oil the barbecue rack. Cook the drumsticks over hot coals if barbecuing, or under a medium-hot grill, for 15 to 20 minutes, turning every 5 minutes. After the last turn, sprinkle the remaining paprika over the drumsticks. Serve immediately.

serves 8
working time 30 mins
total time 3 hours 30 mins
(includes marinating)

calories 160
total fat 6 g   saturated fat 2 g

Meat supplies protein and vitamins and minerals and is also an important source of iron. Meat also contains a high proportion of saturated fats so it's best not to include it in every meal and not to overdo the portion sizes. It's a healthier, as well as cheaper, choice to fill up on vegetables and rice or pasta.

Cheaper cuts are perfect for stewing and casseroling as slow cooking makes sure even tougher cuts of meat will be soft and cooked through. For quick roasting (whether it's for beef, lamb or pork) you need to use a hot oven, for slow roasting a moderate one. Small cuts of meats (e.g. chops and cutlets) can be grilled, while joints of meat are best roasted or casseroled. Mince (either meat, pork or lamb) is probably the most versatile form of meat as it can be used to make anything from meatballs and lasagne to stuffed vegetables. Once again look out for supermarket offers on meat, in particular, it can mean a big saving. Also check out the frozen chests as often 'specials' can mean that some cuts are being offered at the same price as chicken.

Here are a selection of recipes that offer a variety of cooking methods. By trying a number of them you'll be able to see the ones that best suit your taste, as well as your lifestyle.

lamb sausages on skewers

600 g (1¹/₄ lb) lean lamb, trimmed of
fat and minced
1 large tomato, seeded and chopped
¹/₄ tsp salt
freshly ground black pepper
1 tsp sugar
1 tbsp red wine vinegar
3 tbsp chopped parsley
1 tbsp chopped fresh oregano
1 egg white
1 tbsp virgin olive oil
30 g (1 oz) dry breadcrumbs
2 spring onions, thinly sliced
¹/₂ tsp capers
125 ml (4 fl oz) plain low-fat yoghurt

Put the tomato, half of the salt, some pepper, the sugar and vinegar into a frying pan set over medium heat. Cook the mixture, stirring frequently, until only about 4 tbsp remain – about 20 minutes. Transfer the mixture to a bowl and let it cool to room temperature.

In a large bowl, combine the minced lamb with 2 tbsp of the parsley, the oregano, egg white, half of the oil, the breadcrumbs, half of the spring onion, the remaining salt and some pepper. Stir the cooled tomato mixture into the lamb mixture and refrigerate until it is thoroughly chilled – about 30 minutes.

If you plan to barbecue the sausages, light the coal about 30 minutes before cooking time. To grill, preheat the grill for 10 minutes.

Divide the lamb mixture into 4 portions and form each one into a sausage shape about 10 cm (4 inches) long. Thread each sausage onto a skewer, keeping the meal pressed firmly in place.

Pour the remaining oil onto a large plate. Lightly coat the sausages by rolling them in the oil. Grill or barbecue, turning the skewers every now and then, until the meat is lightly browned – 8 to 10 minutes.

Meanwhile, chop the parsley, spring onions and capers. Transfer into a small bowl, and whisk in the yoghurt and some pepper. Serve immediately, passing the sauce separately.

serves 4
working time 30 mins
total time 1 hour 10 mins

calories 245
total fat 11 g
saturated fat 4 g

lamb and mushroom burgers

500 g (1 lb) lean lamb, trimmed of
fat and minced
3 tbsp fresh wholemeal
breadcrumbs
2 tbsp fresh orange juice
1/4 tsp finely grated lemon rind
1 tbsp chopped parsley
2 tsp finely cut chives
1/8 tsp dried marjoram
1/8 tsp salt
freshly ground black pepper
125 g (4 oz) button mushrooms,
chopped
4 granary baps, split in half
carrot ribbons, shredded cabbage,
flat leaf parsley, for garnish

mustard sauce:
1 tbsp grainy mustard
4 tbsp fromage frais
1 tbsp finely cup chives
freshly ground black pepper

serves 4
working time 30 mins
total time 1 hour 5 mins

calories 350
total fat 10 g
saturated fat 5 g

Put the lamb, breadcrumbs, orange juice, lemon rind, parsley, chives, marjoram, salt and some pepper in a bowl and mix the thoroughly by hand. Set the bowl aside. Heat a nonstick frying pan, brush with oil and add the mushrooms, and sauté them over a high heat for 3 minutes, stirring constantly. Allow to cool, then add to the meat mixture. Shape the mixture into 4 burgers, each about 10 cm (4 inches) in diameter. Cover and refrigerate for 30 minutes.

Meanwhile, combine the ingredients for the mustard sauce in a mixing bowl. Set aside.

Preheat the grill to hot, and cook the burgers for about 4 minutes on each side for medium meat. Toast the baps on the cut sides. Place each burger on the bottom half of a bap, garnish with the carrot, celery, cabbage and parsley, spoon on a portion of the mustard sauce and top with the other half of the bap.

hints and tips

If you don't have wholemeal bread then use white or brown for breadcrumbs.

lamb and courgette pie

500 g (1 lb) lean lamb, trimmed of
fat and cut into 5 mm (^{1}/4 inch) dice

1 tbsp virgin olive oil

1 large onion, finely chopped

2 garlic cloves

250 g (8 oz) carrots, cut into 5 mm
(^{1}/4 inch) dice

30 g (1 oz) plain flour

^{1}/4 litre (8 fl oz) chicken stock

1 tsp mixed dried herbs

^{1}/2 tsp salt

freshly ground black pepper

5 sheets filo pastry, each 45 x 30 cm
(18 x 12 inches)

30 g (1 oz) margarine, melted

serves 6
working time 1 hour
total time 2 hours 25 mins

calories 240
total fat 12 g
saturated fat 4 g

Heat the oil in a large sauté pan over medium heat. Add the onion, garlic and carrots. Reduce the heat to low and cook gently until the vegetables are soft but not brown – 10 to 15 minutes. Increase the heat to high, then add the diced lamb. Stir with a wooden spoon until the lamb changes colour – 1 to 2 minutes. Add the courgettes, stir in the flour, stock, mixed herbs, salt and pepper. Bring to the boil, stirring. Reduce the heat to low, cover the pan and simmer until the courgettes are soft – 8 to 10 minutes. Remove the pan from the heat and allow the lamb mixture to cool for about 45 minutes. Preheat the oven to 220°C (425°F or Mark 7). Pour the mixture into a 20 cm (8 inch) pie plate.

Cut four of the filo sheets in half, widthwise. Brush the edge of the pie plate with a little cold water, then cover the meat mixture with one of the half filo sheets, brush the filo with a little of the melted margarine and cover it with another sheet of filo. Using scissors, cut the pastry to fit the dish.

Fold the remaining sheet of filo into four, trim the edges, then cut it lengthwise into two strips and cut these into diamond shapes. Brush the top of the pie with the margarine, then decorate it with the filo diamonds, brushing them individually with the margarine so they stay in place. Make a small hole in the centre of the pie to allow the steam to escape.

Place the pie on a baking sheet and cook it in the oven until the pastry is golden brown – 35 to 40 minutes. Serve immediately.

ULTIMATE
budget cookbook

lamb-stuffed onions

350 g (12 oz) lean lamb, minced

4 large Spanish onions

125 g (4 oz) celeriac, peeled and finely chopped

60 g (2 oz) button mushrooms, chopped

1 tsp chopped fresh marjoram or $1/4$ tsp dried marjoram

4 tbsp grated horseradish

30 g (1 oz) cashew nuts, chopped

$1/4$ tsp salt

freshly ground black pepper

celery leaves, for garnish

Peel the onions, trimming off the root ends, but leaving the tops intact. Place them in a large pan of simmering water and cook them until they are soft but still keep their shape – about 10 minutes. Drain and cool. Slice lids off the pointed ends, about quarter of the way down each onion. Push out the centres of the onions with a teaspoon, leaving shells about two layers thick.

Preheat the oven to 180°C (350°F or Mark 4). Lightly brush a non-stick frying pan with oil and heat it over high heat. Add the lamb, stirring until it changes colour – about 2 minutes. Add the celeriac, mushrooms and marjoram, reduce the heat to medium and cook for a further 2 minutes. Stir in the horseradish, cashew nuts, salt and some pepper and remove the pan from the heat.

Place the onion shells in a shallow ovenproof dish. Using a teaspoon, pack the lamb mixture into the shells, piling it up above the shells if necessary. Place the lids beside the onions. Cover the dish with tinfoil and bake until the onions are tender – about 40 minutes. Replace the lids and serve the onions garnished with celery leaves.

serves 4
working time 30 mins
total time 1 hour 10 mins

calories 215
total fat 10 g
saturated fat 3 g

moussaka

500 g (1 lb) lean lamb, trimmed of
fat and minced
2 garlic cloves, crushed
500 g (1 lb) ripe tomatoes, roughly
chopped
200 ml (7 fl oz) red wine
2 tbsp tomato purée
1 green chilli, halved, seeded and
finely chopped
2 tbsp chopped parsley
1 tbsp chopped fresh marjoram, or
$^1/_2$ tsp dried marjoram
1 bay leaf
$^1/_4$ tsp freshly grated nutmeg
$^3/_4$ tsp salt
freshly ground black pepper
750 g (1$^1/_2$ lb) aubergines, thinly
sliced
250 g (8 oz) potatoes, thinly sliced
30 g (1 oz) grated Parmesan cheese

serves 6
working time 1 hour 10 mins
total time 2 hours 30 mins

calories 380
total fat 14 g
saturated fat 6 g

white sauce:
60 g (2 oz) margarine
60 g (2 oz) plain flour
300 ml ($^1/_2$ pint) milk
$^1/_2$ tsp freshly grated nutmeg
$^1/_8$ tsp salt
300 ml ($^1/_2$ pint) plain low-fat yoghurt

Lightly brush a non-stick frying pan with oil and heat it over medium heat. Add the minced lamb and cook it, stirring constantly, until it changes colour – 3 to 4 minutes. Add the onions and continue stirring for a further 5 minutes. Add the garlic, tomatoes, wine, tomato purée, chilli pepper, marjoram, bay leaf and nutmeg. Season with $^1/_4$ tsp of the salt and some freshly ground black pepper. Continue stirring until the mixture comes to the boil, then reduce the heat, cover and simmer gently for 40 minutes.

Meanwhile, sprinkle the aubergine slices with the remaining $^1/_4$ tsp of the salt. Leave to stand for 20 minutes, then rinse under cold running water to remove the salt.

Pour enough water into a pan to fill it 2.5 cm (1 inch) deep. Set a vegetable steamer in the pan and bring the water to the boil. Put the aubergine slices in the steamer, cover the saucepan tightly and steam the aubergines until tender – about 10 minutes. While they are steaming, boil the potato slices in unsalted water until tender – about 5 minutes. Drain well.

Preheat the oven to 180°C (350°F or Mark 4). Cover the bottom of a 28 x 22 cm (11 x 9 inch) baking dish with the potato slices. Cover the potatoes with half of the aubergines, then add the meat mixture. Arrange the remaining aubergine slices in a layer on top.

To make the sauce, melt the margarine in a pan over medium heat, add the flour and stir for 1 minute. Gradually add the milk, stirring continuously, then add the nutmeg and the salt. Continue stirring the sauce until it thickens – 3 to 4 minutes. Remove from the heat and stir in the yoghurt.

Pour the sauce over the moussaka, then sprinkle on the Parmesan cheese. Bake the moussaka until golden-brown and bubbling – 40 to 50 minutes. Serve hot, straight from the dish.

layered meat loaf

850 g (1³/4 lb) topside of beef, minced

500 g (1 lb) tomatoes, skinned, seeded and chopped

1 onion, chopped

3 garlic cloves, finely chopped

1¹/2 tsp chopped fresh oregano, or ¹/2 tsp dried

125 ml (4 fl oz) port or Madeira

2 tbsp red wine vinegar

1 tbsp sugar

¹/4 tsp salt

freshly ground black pepper

6 tbsp freshly grated Parmesan cheese

60 g (2 oz) dry breadcrumbs

1 egg white

1 tbsp safflower oil

2 bunches watercress, trimmed

1 tbsp fresh thyme or 1 tsp dried

serves 8
working time 40 mins
total time 2 hours

calories 220
total fat 8 g
saturated fat 3 g

Heat a large frying pan over medium-high heat. Put in the tomatoes, onion, garlic and oregano. Cook, stirring occasionally, for 5 minutes. Add the port or Madeira, vinegar, sugar, ¹/8 tsp salt and some pepper. Cook the mixture until almost all of the liquid has evaporated – about 10 minutes. Purée the mixture and place all but 4 tablespoons of it in a large bowl. Preheat the oven to 200°C (400°F or Mark 6).

Add the beef, 4 tbsp of the cheese, half the breadcrumbs, the remaining salt, pepper and the egg white to the tomato mixture in the bowl. Mix well and set the meat aside while you prepare the watercress.

Heat the oil in a large frying pan over high heat. Add the watercress, thyme and some pepper. Cook, stirring constantly, until the watercress has wilted and almost all of the liquid has evaporated – 3 to 4 minutes. Chop the watercress finely. Place it in a bowl and combine it with the remaining breadcrumbs.

To layer the meat loaf, divide the beef mixture into three portions. Using a rolling pin, flatten each portion into a rectangle 12.5 cm (5 inches) wide, 20 cm (8 inches) long and 2 cm (³/4 inch) thick.

Place one rectangle in a shallow baking pan. Top it with half of the watercress mixture, spreading the watercress evenly over the surface. Lay another rectangle on top and cover it with the remaining watercress. Finish with the final rectangle, then spread the reserved tomato sauce over the top and sides of the loaf. Sprinkle the remaining 2 tbsp of Parmesan cheese and bake the meat loaf for 1 hour and 10 minutes. Let the meat loaf stand for 10 minutes, then transfer it to a platter, slice it and serve.

chunky beef chilli

2 large dried mild chilli peppers, seeded and quartered

2 fresh hot chilli peppers, seeded and coarsely chopped

2 tbsp safflower oil

1 kg (2 lb) braising steak, cut into 1 cm ($1/2$ inch) chunks

2 large onions, finely chopped

2 sticks celery, chopped

2 garlic cloves, finely chopped

2 tbsp finely chopped fresh ginger

1 tbsp ground cumin

1 tbsp dried oregano

$1/4$ tsp cayenne pepper

$1/4$ tsp freshly ground black pepper

1 tbsp plain flour

400 g (14 oz) canned tomatoes, chopped with their juice

1 bay leaf

$1 1/2$ tsp salt

$1/2$ tsp grated orange rind

Put the dried mild chillies into a small pan. Pour in 1 litre ($1^3/4$ pints) of water and boil for 5 minutes. Turn off the heat and let the chillies soften for 5 minutes. Transfer them to a blender with 125 ml (4 fl oz) of their soaking liquid (reserve the remaining liquid). Add the fresh chilli peppers and pureé until the mixture is very smooth. Strain the pureé through a sieve into the reserved soaking liquid, rub the solids through with a spoon.

Heat $1/2$ tablespoon of the oil in a large frying pan over medium-high heat. Add $1/4$ of the beef chunks and cook them, turning frequently, until they are browned all over – 8 minutes. Transfer the browned beef to a large pan. Brown the rest of the meat in the same way, using all but the tablespoon of oil in the process.

Add the last $1/2$ tablespoon of oil to the frying pan, with the onions, celery and garlic. Sauté the vegetables for 5 minutes, stirring frequently. Stir in the ginger, cumin, oregano, cayenne pepper and black pepper and cook for 1 minute. Add the flour and cook for 1 more minute, stirring constantly. Transfer the mixture to the pan.

Pour the reserved chilli mixture and $1/2$ litre (16 fl oz) of water into the pan. Stir in the tomatoes and their juice, along with the bay leaf, salt and orange rind. Cook the mixture, over very low heat, until the meat is tender – 2 $1/2$ to 3 hours. Do not allow the mixture to boil. If the chilli gets too thick, add water until it reaches the desired consistency.

serves 8
working time 1 hour
total time 4 hours

calories 230
total fat 10 g
saturated fat 3 g

skewered meatballs with aubergine relish

1.1 kg (2¼ lb) minced topside of
beef
1 kg (2 lb) aubergines, pierced in
several places
2 finely chopped onions
6 garlic cloves, finely chopped
1 tsp olive oil
4 tbsp chopped fresh mint or
2 tsp dried oregano
3 tbsp fresh lemon juice
¼ tsp salt
freshly ground black pepper
2 slices wholemeal bread
5 tbsp chopped parsley
125 ml (4 fl oz) plain low-fat yoghurt

Preheat the oven to 240°C (475°F or Mark 9).

Roast the aubergines in the oven, turning occasionally, until they are blistered on all sides – about 20 minutes. Transfer to a bowl, cover it with clingfilm and refrigerate.

Simmer the onion, garlic, oil and 4 tbsp of water in a pan until the onion is translucent – about 5 minutes. Increase the heat and boil the mixture until the water has evaporated – approximately 1 minute.

To prepare the relish, peel the skin from the aubergines and purée the flesh in a blender. Remove 4 tablespoons of the purée and set it aside. In a small bowl, combine the rest of the aubergine with the chopped mint or oregano, lemon juice, half the onion and garlic mixture, ⅛ tsp of the salt and a generous grinding of pepper. Put the aubergine relish into the fridge.

Soak the bread for 3 minutes in enough water to cover them. Gently squeeze the water from the bread.

Mix the minced beef, moist bread, parsley, the rest of the onion and garlic mixture, the reserved aubergine purée, the remaining salt and freshly ground black pepper. Form the meat mixture into 48 meatballs. Thread three meatballs on each of 16 skewers and set the on a baking sheet. Cook the meatballs in the oven until brown – 10 to 15 minutes.

Arrange the meatballs on a platter and, if you like, garnish with sprigs of mint. Pass the relish and yoghurt separately.

serves 8
working time 1 hour
total time 1 hour 30 mins

calories 235
total fat 7 g
saturated fat 2 g

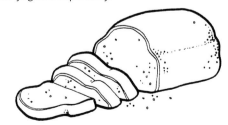

ULTIMATE
budget cookbook

mediterranean meat loaf

1 kg (2 lb) minced topside of beef
1 tsp olive oil
1 small onion, grated
2 sticks celery, finely chopped
2 onions, finely chopped
500 g (1 lb) aubergine, finely chopped
1 sweet red pepper, seeded and finely chopped
8 garlic cloves, finely chopped
6 large ripe tomatoes, skinned, seeded and chopped
4 tbsp finely chopped fresh oregano or 4 tsp dried oregano
135 g (4^1/2 oz) fresh breadcrumbs
2 tbsp currants (optional)
20 preserved vine leaves (optional)

Heat a large frying pan over medium heat. Add oil, celery, onions, aubergine, peppers and garlic. Cook the mixture until the vegetables are soft – about 8 minutes.

Add the tomatoes and oregano to the pan. Increase the heat to medium high and bring the liquid to a simmer, then simmer the tomatoes for 2 minutes. Remove half the mixture and set it aside.

Continue cooking the mixture in the pan until the liquid has evaporated – about 10 minutes. Scrape the vegetables into a large bowl and let them cool slightly. Add the beef, breadcrumbs and currants. Knead the mixture to incorporate the ingredients.

Preheat the oven to 180°C (350°F or Mark 4).

Line a 3 litre (5 pint) ring mould with the vine leaves.

Spoon the meat mixture into the mould, patting it down to release trapped air. Trim any protruding leaves.

Bake the loaf for about 1 hour. After about 50 minutes, reheat the reserved vegetable mixture over medium heat. Invert a serving plate on top of the mould. turn both over, then gently lift off the mould. Fill the space in the centre of the meat loaf with some of the hot vegetables and spoon the rest into a bowl.

serves 10
working time 1 hour
total time 2 hours

calories 220
total fat 6 g
saturated fat 2 g

beef and potato pie

600 g (¹/₄ lb) minced topside of beef
1 kg (2 lb) potatoes, peeled and quartered
2 tbsp skimmed milk
2 tbsp chopped parsley
¹/₄ tsp salt
4 tsp safflower oil
3 tbsp plain flour
¹/₂ litres (16 fl oz) chicken stock
115 g (4 oz) shallots, thinly sliced
90 g (3 oz) dried apples, chopped
2 tbsp cider vinegar
1 tbsp fresh thyme or 1tsp dried thyme
freshly ground black pepper

Preheat the oven to 230°C (450°F or Mark 8).

Place the potatoes in a pan and add enough water to cover them. Boil the water, then reduce the heat and simmer the potatoes until they are tender – 15 to 20 minutes. Drain the potatoes, spread them out on a baking sheet, and place them in the oven to dry. After 5 minutes, remove the pan from the oven and purée the potatoes by working them through a sieve. Combine the potatoes with the milk, parsley and salt and set them aside.

Blend 2 tsp of the oil and the flour in a pan over a low heat and cook the paste for 1 minute. Gradually whisk in the stock and simmer slowly over a low heat until it thickens – about 2 minutes. Remove from heat.

Place the shallots, apples and vinegar in a frying pan and cook them over a medium heat until the vinegar has evaporated and the shallots are limp – about 2 minutes. Add the beef and brown it over high heat, breaking up any whole pieces as you do so. Remove from the heat and stir in the thyme, some freshly ground black pepper and the thickened stock.

Divide the meat mixture evenly between 4 small gratin dishes or place it in one large dish. Top the meat with the potato mixture, smooth the surface with a spatula and flute the potatoes using the edge of the spatula. Brush the surface with the remaining 2 tsp of oil. Bake the beef and potatoe pie until it lightly browns – 20 to 30 minutes.

serves 4
working time 1 hour
total time 2 hours

calories 485
total fat 12 g
saturated fat 3 g

burghul-stuffed red peppers

350 g (12 oz) minced topside of beef

4 large red or green peppers

4 tsp olive oil

1 onion, chopped

2 tsp fresh thyme or $1/2$ tsp dried thyme

125 g (4 oz) mushrooms, thinly sliced

2 tbsp finely chopped celery

125 g (4 oz) burghul

$1/4$ tsp salt

freshly ground black pepper

350 ml (12 fl oz) chicken stock

1 garlic clove, finely chopped

2 tbsp red wine vinegar

Preheat the oven to 200°C (400°F or Mark 6).

To prepare the peppers, cut and discard their stems. Slice off the peppers' tops, dice them and set the pieces aside. Seed and de-rib the peppers. Heat 1 tbsp of the oil in a pan over medium heat. Add half of the onion, half of the thyme, the mushrooms, celery, burghul, $1/8$ tsp of the salt and some pepper. Cook the vegetables and burghul, stirring frequently, for 5 minutes. Add the stock, stir the mixture well, and cover the pan. Cook the mixture, stirring occasionally, until the liquid is absorbed – 12 minutes.

In a frying pan, heat the remaining oil over medium-high heat. When the pan is hot, add the beef, the diced peppers, the remaining onion, the remaining thyme and the garlic. Cook, stirring frequently, until the beef is browned – 5 to 7 minutes. Add the remaining salt, some freshly ground black pepper and the vinegar. Cook for 30 seconds, then remove it form the heat.

Combine the burghul mixture with the beef and fill the peppers, mounding the filling. Bake the stuffed peppers in a shallow casserole, for 25 minutes. Allow the peppers to stand for 5 minutes before serving.

serves 4
working time 25 mins
total time 45 mins

calories 280
total fat 7 g
saturated fat 2 g

meat and tomato loaf

2 tbsp olive oil

2 onions, finely chopped

400 g (14 oz) canned plum tomatoes, chopped

1 tbsp fresh oregano or 1 tsp dried

$1/4$ tsp salt

freshly ground black pepper

750 g ($1^1/_2$ lb) mince

3 garlic cloves

30 g (1 oz) parsley

1 tsp Tabasco

2 tsp Worcester sauce

175 g (6 oz) dry breadcrumbs

1 egg

Heat 1 tbsp of the oil in a pan over medium-low heat. Add half of the onion, stir, then cover and cook the onion until it has softened – about 5 minutes. Add tomatoes, oregano, salt and pepper. Simmer uncovered, stirring occasionally, until it has reduced to about 300 ml ($1/2$ pint) – about 40 minutes. Sieve.

Preheat the oven to 180°C (350°F or Mark 4). Brush a loaf tin with some of the olive oil.

Put the mince in a bowl with the tomato sauce. Mix in the garlic, onion, parsley, Tabasco and Worcester sauce, and plenty of freshly ground black pepper. Add the breadcrumbs and mix well. Finally, add the egg and blend thoroughly into the mixture.

Form the mixture into a smooth fat sausage shape and lay it in the tin, pressing it down firmly on all sides. Brush the top of the loaf with the remaining oil then cover it with foil. Bake until cooked through and a skewer inserted into the middle is hot to touch when withdrawn – about an hour.

Leave the loaf to cool at room temperature – about 2 hours – refrigerate for at least 4 hours before serving.

serves 8
working time 20 mins
total time 8 hours (inc chilling)

calories 285
total fat 12 g
saturated fat 4 g

hints and tips

Try serving with crusty bread for a tasty supper.

afghan noodles

250 g (8 oz) curly egg noodles
$^1/_4$ litre (8 fl oz) low-fat yoghurt
4 tbsp chopped fresh mint or 2 tbsp
dried mint
$2^1/_2$ tsp chilli powder
1 tbsp fresh lemon juice
1 tbsp safflower oil
1 onion, finely chopped
500 g (1 lb) lean minced beef
$^1/_2$ tsp salt
1 ripe tomato, skinned, seeded and
chopped
15 g ($^1/_2$ oz) butter

To prepare the sauce, combine the yoghurt with $^3/_4$ of the mint, $^1/_2$ tsp chilli powder and the lemon juice.

Heat the oil in a frying pan, over medium-high heat. Add the onion, and sauté for 3 minutes. Add the beef, the remaining chilli powder and the salt, and cook for 6 minutes, stirring frequently. Stir in the tomato and cook for 2 minutes more.

Cook the egg noodles in 3 litres (5 pints) of salted boiling water, until they are al dente – about 9 minutes. Drain the noodles and return them to the pan. Add the butter and stir gently until it melts and the noodles are coated.

To serve, transfer the hot noodles to a warm serving plate. Pour the sauce over the noodles in a ring 5 cm (2 inch) in from the edge of the noodles, then arrange the beef mixture in the centre of the ring. Sprinkle the remaining mint over the top, and serve.

serves 6
working time 35 mins
total time 45 mins

calories 350
total fat 12 g
saturated fat 5 g

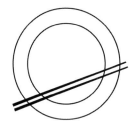

bacon and onion potato salad

1 kg (2 lb) small red potatoes,
scrubbed
2 bacon rashers, cut into thin strips
1 red onion, thinly sliced
4 tbsp finely chopped celery
1 tbsp cornflour, mixed with 125 ml
(4 fl oz) chicken stock
4 tbsp white wine vinegar
freshly ground black pepper
2 tbsp chopped parsley

Prick the potatoes with a fork in two places. Arrange them in a circle on paper towel in the microwave oven. Cook them on high for 7 minutes. Turn the potatoes over and continue cooking them on high until they are barely soft – 5 to 7 minutes. Remove the potatoes from the oven and set aside until they are cool enough to handle.

Put the bacon in a bowl. Cover the bowl with paper towel and microwave on high for 2 minutes. Remove the towel and drain off the excess fat, then add the onion and celery to the bowl. Toss the bacon and vegetables together, cover the bowl, and microwave on high for 90 seconds. Stir in the cornflour mixture and vinegar. Cover the bowl and microwave it on high until the dressing thickens slightly – about 2 minutes.

Cut the potatoes into slices about 5 mm ($^1/_4$ inch) thick. Pour the dressing over the potato slices. Add a grinding of pepper and half the parsley. Toss the salad, then cool. Scatter the rest of the parsley on top just before serving.

serves 6
working time 10 mins
total time 20 mins

calories 140
total fat 2 g
saturated fat 0 g

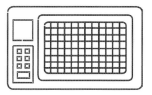

ULTIMATE
budget cookbook

pork kofta

500 g (1 lb) minced pork fillet
1 lemon, grated rind only
2 crushed garlic cloves
1 tbsp coriander seeds, toasted and ground
$1/2$ tsp salt
freshly ground black pepper
3 tbsp dry white wine
$1^1/2$ tbsp fresh lemon juice
$1^1/2$ tbsp virgin olive oil
4 grated carrots
30 g (1 oz) fresh coriander leaves, chopped
4 pitta breads

Combine the pork with the lemon rind, garlic, coriander seeds, salt and some pepper. Divide into 4 and roll into sausage shapes, about 15 x 2.5cm (6 x 1 inch). Place the kofta in a shallow dish and pour on the wine, 1 tbsp of the lemon juice and the oil. Leave to marinate for at least 2 hours, turning the kofta at frequent intervals.

Preheat the grill to high. Mix the carrots with the coriander leaves and the remaining lemon juice.

Remove the kofta from the marinade and grill them until the pork feels firm and is well browned on all sides – about 7 minutes. Meanwhile, warm the pitta bread through in a 170°C (325°F or Mark 3) oven.

When the kofta are cooked, slit open one side of each pitta bread to make a pocket. Fill with a quarter of the carrot salad and one hot kofta.

serves 4
working time 35 mins
total time 2 hours 30 mins (inc marinating)

calories 375
total fat 20 g   saturated fat 5 g

pork risotto

350 g (12 oz) pork fillet, cut into cubes

1 tbsp virgin olive oil

1 onion, finely chopped

1 garlic clove, crushed

125 g (4 oz) button mushrooms, chopped

$1/2$ tsp chopped fresh sage

250 g (8 oz) ground black grain rice

$1/2$ tsp salt

freshly ground black pepper

300 ml ($1/2$ pint) dry white wine

125 g (4 oz) shelled peas, blanched in boiling water, or frozen peas

1 tbsp grated Parmesan cheese

3 tbsp flat-leaf parsley, torn into small pieces

Heat the olive oil in a pan over medium heat and brown the cubes of meat. Stir in the onion and continue cooking until the onion begins to turn golden at the edges. Add the garlic, mushrooms, and sage. When the mushrooms are wilting, increase the heat, add the rice, salt and some pepper, and stir for a couple of minutes.

Mix the wine with an equal amount of water and pour half of the liquid into the pan. Reduce the heat and stir, while bringing the liquid to a simmer. Stir the mixture frequently as the liquid is absorbed – 5 to 10 minutes.

Pour in the rest of the liquid and the peas, bring back to a simmer, and stir. Cover the pan and leave to cook very slowly, stirring from time to time until the mixture is creamy but not mushy – 10 to 15 minutes. Just before serving, stir in the cheese and parsley.

serves 4
working time 25 mins
total time 40 mins

calories 460
total fat 12 g
saturated fat 4 g

hints and tips

To turn this into a vegetarian dish just replace the pork with one or two of your favourite vegetables.

ULTIMATE
budget cookbook

pitta pork balls

250 g (8 oz) pork loin, minced
125 g (4 oz) burghul
2 tsp safflower oil
1 onion, finely chopped
1 garlic clove, crushed
2 tsp curry powder
$1/2$ tsp ground coriander
$1/4$ tsp ground cinnamon
$1/4$ tsp salt
6 wholemeal pitta breads
8 cos lettuce leaves, finely shredded

yoghurt dressing:
80 ml (3 fl oz) plain low-fat yoghurt
1 tbsp chopped fresh mint
1 tbsp fresh lemon juice
cayenne pepper

Preheat the oven to 190°C (375°F or Mark 5). In a bowl, soak the burghul in 300 ml ($1/2$ pint) of boiling water for 15 minutes to swell and absorb the liquid.

Meanwhile, heat the oil in a small pan. Add the onion and garlic and cook very gently for 3 minutes, stirring occasionally. Add the curry powder, coriander and cinnamon, and cook gently for 2 minutes.

Add the onion mixture, pork and salt to the soaked burghul and mix thoroughly. Form the mixture into 12 neat oval balls, about 1.5 cm ($3/4$ inch) thick and 7.5 cm (3 inches) long. Place the balls onto a lightly greased baking sheet and cook in the oven for 35 minutes, turning halfway through cooking time.

Meanwhile, make the dressing. In a bowl, mix the yoghurt with the mint and lemon juice, and season with some cayenne pepper. Refrigerate until needed.

Warm the pitta breads under a medium grill for 1 minute on each side, then slit along one side of each bread, to form a pocket. Half fill each pocket with some of the shredded lettuce leaves. Spoon a little yoghurt dressing into each bread and arrange two hot pork cakes on top. Fill the sides of the pitas with a little more lettuce, and add some slices of cucumber and tomato to each one. Top the filling with a spoonful of the remaining dressing. Serve at once.

serves 6
working and total time 1 hour

calories 230
total fat 6 g
saturated fat 2 g

hints and tips

Keep a bottle of lemon juice in the fridge, excellent for dressings or with fish, if you can't get fresh lemons.

pork balls with angel's hair pasta

250 g (8 oz) pork, minced
1 tsp fennel seeds
2 tbsp finely chopped parsley
1 tsp fresh lemon juice
$^1/_4$ tsp salt
freshly ground black pepper
1 bay leaf
1 carrot
10 black pepper corns
300 ml ($^1/_2$ pint) dry white wine
2 fennel bulbs, tops attached
150 g (5 oz) angel's hair pasta
30 g (1 oz) butter
1 tbsp grated Parmesan cheese

Combine the pork, fennel seeds, parsley and lemon juice, and season lightly with the salt and some pepper. Set the mixture aside.

To make a vegetable stock, put the bay leaf, onion, carrot, peppercorns and wine in a pan and cover with water. Bring to the boil, then reduce the heat to a simmer.

While the stock is simmering, wash the fennel and slice it very thinly. Chop the feathery tips finely and reserve for garnishing. Form the pork mixture into balls about the size of large marbles.

When the vegetable liquid has simmered for at least 10 minutes, plunge the fennel into the pan and simmer until it is cooked, but still a little crunchy. Strain the contents of the pan. Reserve the fennel and the liquid and discard the other ingredients. Return the liquid to the pan, and add the pork balls.

Bring a large pan of water to the boil. Throw in the pasta and cook it until al dente — about 4 minutes.

When the pork balls are cooked — about 5 minutes — add the fennel for a few seconds to warm through. Strain the pork and fennel, reserving about 4 tbsp of the cooking liquid. Strain the pasta. Melt the butter in the larger pan, and add the pork, fennel and pasta. Divide the mixture among 4 warmed plates, pour a tablespoon of the reserved cooking liquid over each serving, and scatter the Parmesan and the reserved fennel fronds over the top. Serve immediately.

serves 4
working and total time 40 mins

calories 280
total fat 12 g
saturated fat 6 g

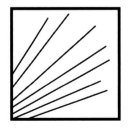

pork and spinach pie

300 g (10 oz) frozen chopped
spinach
250 g (8 oz) chopped pork fillet
1 tsp fennel seeds
2 garlic cloves, finely chopped
1 tsp ground coriander
$^1/_8$ tsp salt
1 tbsp virgin olive oil
$^1/_2$ tsp dried hot red pepper flakes
600 ml (1 pint) buttermilk
1 egg, plus 1 egg white
1 French bread loaf, cut into 1 cm
($^1/_2$ inch) slices
60 g (2 oz) Parmesan cheese

Microwave the spinach on high for $2^1/_2$ minutes to defrost. Set aside.

Mix together the pork, fennel seeds, garlic, coriander, salt, $^1/_2$ tbsp of oil and $^1/_4$ tsp of pepper flakes. In another bowl, mix the buttermilk, egg and egg white, the remaining oil and pepper flakes.

Spread the bread slices in a single layer on the bottom of a shallow baking tray. Pour on all but 4 tbsp of the buttermilk mixture, then turn the slices. Let the bread stand, turning the slices frequently until they have absorbed nearly all the liquid – about 15 minutes.

Microwave the pork mixture on high for $1^1/_2$ minutes, stirring the mixture once at midpoint.

Remove the spinach from the package and squeeze to remove as much liquid as possible. Stir the spinach into the pork mixture, along with the reserved 4 tbsp of the buttermilk mixture and about half the cheese. Spoon about a quarter of the pork mixture into a 28 cm (11 inch) glass pie dish. Arrange half of the bread slices in a close-fitting layer on top of the pork. Repeat and pour on any remaining buttermilk mixture. Cover the dish.

Microwave on medium for 4 minutes. Rotate and cook for another 4 minutes. Uncover and scatter the remaining cheese over the top. Cook the dish 8 minutes more. Let the dish stand for at least 5 minutes before serving it.

serves 6
working time 30 mins
total time 1 hour

calories 300
total fat 11 g
saturated fat 4 g

pork and salsify pie

500 g (1 lb) lean pork, cut into pieces
150 ml ($^1/_4$ pint) dry white wine
3 garlic cloves, crushed
1 small onion, quartered
2 fresh bay leaves and thyme sprigs
$^1/_4$ tsp salt
freshly ground black pepper
$^1/_2$ lemon
250 g (8 oz) salsify
300 ml ($^1/_2$ pint) unsalted vegetable stock
8 baby onions
125 g (4 oz) tomatoes, skinned and chopped
1 tbsp capers, chopped
$^1/_2$ tsp green peppercorns
1 tsp arrowroot, mixed with 1 tbsp stock or water

serves 6
working time 1 hour
total time 4 hours 15 mins
(inc marinating)

calories 340
total fat 17 g   saturated fat 8 g

pastry dough:
175 g (6 oz) plain flour
$^1/_4$ tsp salt
45 g ($1^1/_2$ oz) unsalted butter, cubed
45 g ($1^1/_2$ oz) white vegetable fat, cubed

Put the pork, wine, garlic, onion, bay leaves, thyme, salt and a little pepper in a dish and leave to marinate for 2 hours.

Sift the flour and salt into a large bowl. Rub in the butter and vegetable fat until the mixture has a coarse texture. Sprinkle on water, knead and press into a ball, then wrap it in plastic film and cook for 15 minutes.

Cook the salsify in boiling water, with lemon juice, until half-tender, then drain.

Put the marinade in a pan, simmer for 30 minutes, skimming. Remove the meat, discard the rest, and add the stock. Return the meat to the pan, add the salsify and baby onions, and simmer for a further 30 minutes.

Preheat the oven to 190°C (375°F or Mark 5). Place a funnel in the centre of a pie dish, add the meat, vegetables, tomatoes, capers and peppercorns. In another pan, bring 300 ml ($^1/_2$ pint) of cooking liquid to the boil with the arrowroot. Simmer to thicken, then pour into the pie dish.

Roll out the dough and place on the dish, leaving a slit for the funnel. Trim and crimp the edges. Bake for 40 minutes and serve hot.

ULTIMATE
budget cookbook

leek and bacon potatoes

4 potatoes, pricked all over
with a fork
60 g (2 oz) lean smoked bacon,
trimmed of fat and diced
125 g (4 oz) leeks, finely chopped
1 tbsp skimmed milk
freshly ground black pepper

Place the potatoes in a circle on paper towel in the microwave. Cook on high for 10 minutes, turning after 5 minutes, then remove them from the oven and set them aside.

Put the bacon and leeks in a small bowl and microwave on high for 3 minutes, stirring once. Cut the tops off the potatoes and scoop out the insides to within 5 mm (^{1}/4 inch) of the skins. Mash the scooped out potato with the milk and season lightly with freshly ground black pepper. Stir in the bacon and leeks. Pile the potato, bacon and leek mixture back into the skins, place the lids on top and reheat on high for 1 to 2 minutes before serving.

serves 4
working time 15 mins
total time 25 mins

calories 145
total fat 2 g
saturated fat trace

pilaff with pig's heart

1 pig's heart
(about 250 g (8oz)), finely diced
2 tbsp virgin olive oil
1 onion, finely chopped
2 tbsp pine nuts
350 g (12 oz) long grain rice
2 tbsp currants
$1/4$ tsp sugar
$1/4$ tsp ground allspice
$1/4$ tsp ground cinnamon
$1/2$ tsp salt
freshly ground black pepper
3 tbsp finely chopped parsley

Heat the olive oil in a large pan over medium heat and sauté the diced heart for about 5 minutes. Add the onion and pine nuts, and cook until both are beginning to colour. Add the rice, and stir to coast well with oil, then stir in $3/4$ litre ($1 1/4$ pints) of water and all the remaining ingredients except the parsley. Bring to the boil, reduce the heat, then cover and simmer for 10 minutes.

Stir in the parsley, re-cover the pan and leave to stand, off the heat, for 15 minutes more. Mix well and serve hot or warm.

serves 6
working time 20 mins
total time 45 mins

calories 565
total fat 15 g
saturated fat 3 g

ULTIMATE
budget cookbook

pork burgers

250 g (8 oz) pork fillet, minced
250 g (8 oz) topside of veal, minced
1 onion, finely chopped
$^1/_4$ tsp salt
$^1/_2$ tsp dry mustard
$^1/_4$ tsp chilli powder
1 tbsp safflower oil
4 wholemeal baps, halved
4 lettuce leaves, washed and dried
4 slices of beef tomato
4 pickled chilli peppers

chilli topping:
4 tbsp chilli relish
1 carrot, grated
2 shallots, finely chopped
2.5 cm (1 inch) piece of cucumber,
finely chopped

In a bowl, mix the pork with the veal, onion, salt, dry mustard and chilli powder. Form the mixture into four burgers, 1 cm ($^1/_2$ inch) thick.

Heat the oil in a frying pan over medium heat. Add the pork burgers and cook them for 5 to 6 minutes on each side.

Meanwhile, make the topping. In a bowl, mix the chilli relish with the carrot, shallots and cucumber. Warm the baps under a medium-hot grill.

Arrange a lettuce leaf on the base of each bap, then add a pork burger to each, and top with a slice of tomato and a spoonful of chilli topping. Cover the bap lids and secure them in position with cocktail sticks. Garnish the burgers with the pickled chilli peppers, and serve at once.

serves 4
total time 35 mins

calories 340
total fat 12 g
saturated fat 4 g

hints and tips

Serve with your choice of side salad or chips.

ham with broad beans

175 g (6 oz) lean ham, diced
750 g (1¹/₂ lb) shelled broad beans
1 tsp safflower oil
1 tbsp plain flour
4 tbsp plain flour
4 tbsp white wine (optional)
freshly ground black pepper
2 tbsp single cream
2 tbsp finely chopped fresh summer savoury or 1¹/₂ tsp dried summer savoury

Bring a pan of water to the boil. Add the broad beans and simmer until they are soft but still resistant – about 5 minutes. Strain them and set aside, reserving the cooking liquid.

Heat the oil in a large pan, add the diced ham and fry gently for 1 minute. Stir in the flour and cook for a further 1 minute, stirring continuously. Add the wine and about 150 ml (¹/₄ pint) of the bean cooking liquid. Simmer the mixture for 2 minutes, adding more cooking liquid if the sauce is too thick. Season with some freshly ground black pepper. Add the cream and allow the liquid to bubble up once.

Stir the beans into the pan, warm through, sprinkle with the summer savoury and serve.

serves 6
working time 15 mins
total time 30 mins

calories 130
total fat 4 g
saturated fat 2 g

ULTIMATE
budget cookbook

pork and apple stew

2 tbsp oil
500 g (1 lb) boneless pork shoulder,
fat trimmed away
3 cooking apples, 2 cut into large
chunks, 1 cored and thinly sliced
1 onion, sliced
1 tsp dried sage
$^1/_4$ tsp salt
$^3/_4$ litre ($1^1/_4$ pints) unsalted stock
1 ripe tomato, skinned, seeded and
chopped

Heat 1 tablespoon of the oil in a heavy-bottomed pan over medium-high heat. Add the pork and onion, and sauté them until the pork is lightly browned and the onion is translucent – about 5 minutes. Add the apple chunks, sage, salt, a generous grinding of pepper and the stock. Reduce the heat to maintain a simmer, then cover the pan and cook the stew until the pork is tender – about 1 hour.

Remove the pork from the pan and set it aside. Carefully skim as much fat from the surface of the liquid as you can. Purée the apple chunks and onion with their cooking liquid in several batches in a food mill. (Alternatively, purée the mixture in a food processor, then press the purée through a fine sieve with a wooden spoon.) Return the purée and the pork to the pan, and heat the stew over medium-high heat.

While the stew is heating, pour the remaining oil into a heavy frying pan over medium-high heat. Add the uncooked apple slices and sauté them until they are lightly browned. Stir them into the stew with the tomatoes and serve at once.

serves 4
working time 30 mins
total time 1 hour 45 mins

calories 280
total fat 12 g
saturated fat 2 g

mexican pork

500 g (1 lb) pork fillet, trimmed of fat and cut into cubes
60 g (2 oz) dried kidney beans, soaked in water overnight
1 tbsp olive oil
1 onion, finely chopped
1 garlic clove, crushed
1 tsp chilli powder
$1/4$ tsp ground allspice
$1^1/2$ tbsp tomato purée
30 ml ($1/2$ pint) unsalted chicken stock
2 tsp arrowroot
$1/2$ tsp salt
2 tbsp soured cream
2 tbsp plain low-fat yoghurt

Drain the kidney beans, place them in a saucepan, cover with water and bring to the boil. Boil rapidly for at least 10 minutes, then reduce the heat, cover and simmer until tender. Drain well.

Heat the oil in a large heavy saucepan; add the pork, onion and garlic and cook for 4 to 5 minutes, stirring frequently to brown.

Stir in the chilli powder, allspice and tomato purée and add the stock. Bring to the boil, then reduce the heat, cover and simmer for 20 minutes.

Add the cooked kidney beans to the pan. In a small bowl, mix the arrowroot with 2 tablespoons of cold water. Add the mixture to the pan and stir well, until the juices are thickened. Season with salt.

Mix together the soured cream and yoghurt. Spoon a quarter of the mixture on to each serving.

Serves 4
Working time 20 mins
Total time 8 hours (includes soaking)

calories 250
total fat 11 g
saturated fat 4 g

minced beef with sweet peppers and pasta

600 g (1^1/$_4$ lb) beef mince
2 sweet red peppers
1 tbsp olive oil
6 garlic cloves, thinly sliced
^{1}/$_4$ tsp salt
freshly ground black pepper
400 g (14 oz) canned chopped
tomatoes, with their juice
6 tbsp red wine vinegar
1 tsp sugar
350 g (12 oz) courgettes, trimmed,
halved lengthwise and cut into
5mm (^{1}/$_4$ inch) pieces
350 g (12 oz) penne or other tubular
pasta
^{1}/$_4$ litre (8 fl oz) unsalted chicken
stock
30 g (1 oz) fresh basil, shredded
4 tbsp freshly grated Parmesan
cheese

Grill the peppers until their skins blister. Transfer to a bowl and cover with plastic film – this helps loosen the skins. When cool, peel and seed them over a bowl to catch any juice. Cut into thin strips and strain the juice.

Heat the oil in a heavy frying pan over medium-high heat. Add the beef, onions, garlic and seasoning. Cook, stirring, until the beef browns. Add the chopped tomatoes and their juice, the vinegar and the sugar. Reduce the heat and simmer the mixture for 10 minutes. Add the courgettes and the peppers and juice, cook the mixture for another 5 minutes.

Meanwhile, cook the pasta for 6 minutes in salted boiling water. Drain and return it to the pan; pour in the stock, cover, and bring to a simmer. Cook the pasta 1 minute longer, then add the beef mixture, basil and plenty of pepper and stir. Simmer, stirring, until most of the liquid is absorbed.

Transfer to a large bowl. Sprinkle on the Parmesan, and serve.

serves 6
working and total time 30 mins

calories 415
total fat 9 g
saturated fat 3 g

potatoes with a spiced lamb stuffing

150 g (5 oz) lamb, mined
8 even-sized potatoes, scrubbed
1 small onion, finely chopped
1 garlic clove, crushed
1 tbsp raisins, rinsed and finely chopped
1 tbsp pinenuts, roughly chopped (optional)
1 tsp ground cinnamon
$1/2$ tsp ground allspice
$1/2$ tsp ground turmeric
2 tbsp tomato purée
$1/4$ tsp salt
freshly ground black pepper
6 tbsp unsalted stock
1 tbsp crème fraiche

Preheat the oven to 200° C (400° F or Mark 6).

Make a deep horizontal slit about one quarter of the way down each potato. Bake them in the oven for about 1 hour.

Meanwhile, make the stuffing. Lightly brush a non-stick frying pan with oil and heat it over medium heat. Stir-fry the onion until it is brown. Add the minced lamb and continue stir-frying until it changes colour, than add the garlic, raisins, pinenuts, cinnamon, allspice, turmeric, tomato purée, salt and some freshly ground pepper. Stir for 1 minute, then add the stock and continue cooking the mixture for a further 5 minutes. Set the stuffing aside.

When the potatoes are cool enough to handle, slice their tops and hollow our their insides with a teaspoon, taking care not to puncture their skins; leave a shell of about 5 mm ($1/4$ inch) on each potato. Mash half of the scooped-out potato with the crème fraîche. Spoon the mashed potato into the potato shells, pressing down in the centre to make a well for the lamb stuffing. Fill the shells with the stuffing and return them to the oven to heat through – about 10 minutes. Serve immediately.

serves 4
working time 40 mins
total time 1 hour 40 mins

calories 270
total fat 5 g
saturated fat 2 g

stir-fried liver in orange sauce

350 g (12 oz) pig's liver, thinly sliced

2 tbsp safflower oil

2 onions, sliced

1 sweet green pepper, seeded and sliced

1 garlic clove, chopped

1 tbsp plain flour

2 tbsp tomato purée

3 oranges – 2 peeled, halved and sliced, juice only of the third

125 ml (4 fl oz) unsalted vegetable stock

$^1/_2$ tsp salt

freshly ground black pepper

3 tbsp single cream (optional)

Heat the oil in a wok or frying pan over high heat and cook the liver until it has coloured – 3 to 4 minutes. Remove the liver from the pan and set it aside while you make the sauce.

Add the sliced onions, green pepper and garlic to the pan and cook over low heat for 5 to 10 minutes to soften them. Stir in the flour and tomato purée, then gradually add the orange juice and vegetable stock.

Season with salt and some freshly ground black pepper and bring to the boil, stirring continuously.

Reserve a few orange slices for a garnish, add the remaining slices of orange to the pan with the cooked liver, and heat through for another minute. Remove the pan from the heat and stir in the cream. Serve the liver garnished with the reserved orange slices.

serves 4
total time 15 mins

calories 340
total fat 18 g
saturated fat 5 g

There's a huge variety of fish available, and although many have very different tastes and textures, all are nutritious as fish is a terrific source of protein, vitamins and minerals.

If you're buying fresh fish make sure that it has bright eyes and scales. It should also have a healthy, pleasant smell — if it smells 'off', unpleasant or, ironically, fishy, it isn't fresh! There are basically three categories of fish: oily (e.g. herring, mackerel, mullet, salmon and trout); white (e.g. haddock, cod, halibut, hake, plaice, skate, whiting and sole) and shellfish (e.g. crab, lobster, shrimps, scampi, prawns, mussels and scallops) although there is also a range of smoked fish, from haddock to salmon.

More inexpensive fish include coley, haddock, herrings, etc although it's worth looking out for special offers at the supermarket as well as the fishmonger. Don't dismiss frozen fish, or the bumper bags of fillets that are often on offer. They can make a quick and tasty dinner but you must leave yourself enough time to defrost thoroughly otherwise you can end up with a very watery, and relatively tasteless, meal!

If you buy from a fishmonger, or a supermarket fish counter, you can always ask for the fish to be cleaned, gutted and filleted. Fish can be served simply by grilling, steaming or baking in the oven, parcel-wrapped, topped with a little fat, lemon and seasoning. Alternatively, try some of the recipes below.

fishcakes with horseradish sauce

350 g (12 oz) cod fillets (or haddock or coley)

125 g (4 oz) dry breadcrumbs

1 egg

1 egg white

125 g (4 oz) onion, finely chopped

4 tbsp chopped parsley or fresh coriander

3 garlic cloves, finely chopped

2 tbsp grainy mustard

2 tbsp anise-flavoured liqueur (optional)

2 tbsp fresh lemon juice

$1^1/_2$ tsp capers, chopped

1 tbsp paprika

$^1/_4$ tsp cayenne pepper

150 ml ($^1/_4$ pint) plain low-fat yoghurt

2 tbsp red wine vinegar

Preheat the oven to 200°C (400°F or Mark 6). With a large knife, finely chop the fish. Put the fish in a large bowl. Add 45 g ($1^1/_2$ oz) of the breadcrumbs, the egg, egg white, onion, all but 1 tbsp of the parsley or coriander, the garlic, 1 tbsp of the mustard, the liqueur, the lemon juice, capers, paprika and cayenne pepper and mix thoroughly.

Put the rest of the breadcrumbs on a shallow bowl. Divide the fish mixture into 8 equal portions. Pat one of the portions into a cake about 2 cm ($^3/_4$ inch) thick. Coat the cake with breadcrumbs and place it on an oiled sheet. Repeat to form the remaining portions into crumbed fishcakes. Bake for 20 minutes.

While they are in the oven, prepare the sauce in a small bowl. Mix the remaining mustard and parsley or coriander with the yoghurt, vinegar and horseradish,

Serve the fishcakes with a dollop of sauce.

serves 4
working time 20 mins
total time 40 mins

calories 180
total fat 4 g
saturated fat 1 g

ULTIMATE
budget cookbook

haddock with endive and bacon

500 g (1 lb) cod fillets (or haddock
or coley)
2 garlic cloves, finely chopped
2 tbsp fresh lemon juice
1 tsp fresh rosemary or $1/4$ tsp dried
rosemary, crumbled
freshly ground black pepper
2 rashers streaky bacon, rind
removed
1 endive (about 500 g (1 lb)), cut
into 2.5 cm (1 inch) pieces
$1/8$ tsp salt

Rinse the haddock under cold water and pat it dry. Cut into 4 serving pieces. Rub the fish with half of the garlic, 1 tbsp of lemon juice, the rosemary and a generous grinding of pepper. Set aside.

Cut the rashers in half crosswise and put in the bottom of a large dish. Microwave on high until done but not crisp – about 2 minutes. Lay a strip of bacon on top of each piece of fish.

Add the rest of the garlic to the bacon fat in the dish. Add the endives, with the remaining lemon juice, salt and pepper. Toss the endives, then mound it in the centre of the dish. Microwave on high for 2 minutes. Briefly toss the endives again, then microwave on high until it wilts – about 2 minutes more.

Lay the fish on top of the endives. Microwave on medium until the flesh is opaque – 5 to 6 minutes. Remove from the oven and spoon the juices that have collected in the bottom into a small pan. Boil the juices rapidly until only 2 tbsp of the liquid remain. Pour the sauce over the fish and serve at once.

serves 4
total time 20 mins

calories 150
total fat 3 g
saturated fat 1 g

hints and tips

To add an eastern twist to this recipe why not replace the endive with pak choi.

baked cod plaki

500 g (1 lb) cod fillets (or haddock,
halibut or coley)
2 large tomatoes, sliced
2 small onions, sliced
1 fennel bulb, cored, sliced
crosswise, feathery tops reserved
2 garlic cloves, finely chopped
1 tbsp chopped fresh oregano, or
2 tsp dried oregano
3 tbsp dry white wine
60 g (2 oz) crumbled feta cheese
2 tbsp chopped fresh parsley
4 oil-cured black olives, stoned and
sliced
freshly ground black pepper

Preheat the oven to 190°C (375°F or Mark 5). Lightly oil a large baking dish, layer the tomatoes, onions, fennel, garlic and oregano in the bottom. Rinse the fish under cold water and pat it dry. Slice the fish crosswise into pieces about 5 cm (2 inch) wide. Arrange the fish on top of the vegetables and sprinkle it with the wine.

Cover the dish and bake until it is opaque and feels firm to the touch – 15 to 20 minutes. Remove from the oven. Sprinkle the fish with the feta cheese, parsley, olives and some pepper. Garnish with some of the fennel tops and serve immediately, spooning the pan juices over each portion.

serves 6
working time 30 mins
total time 45 mins

calories 150
total fat 5 g
saturated fat 3 g

ULTIMATE
budget cookbook

stuffed herrings

4 herrings, dressed
15 g ($^{1}/_{2}$ oz) unsalted butter
1 onion, finely chopped
175 g (6 oz) mushrooms, chopped
1 lemon, rind only, finely grated
1 tbsp lemon juice
1 tbsp chopped parsley
1 tsp fresh thyme leaves
60 g (2 oz) fresh white breadcrumbs
$^{1}/_{4}$ tsp salt
freshly ground black pepper

garnish:
sliced mushrooms
parsley
lemon wedges

Preheat the oven to 200°C (400°F or Mark 6).

Wash the herrings thoroughly then pat them dry. To remove the bones, take one fish at a time and place it on a work surface, belly down. Gently but firmly, press along the length of the backbone to flatten the fish. Turn the herring over, and run a thumb under the bones at each side of the backbone to loosen. Lift the bones out in one piece and snip the bone 2.5 cm (1 inch) from the tail.

Melt the butter in a frying pan, add the onion, and cook for 4 to 5 mins. Add the mushrooms and cook for 3 to 4 mins until they are softened. Stir in the lemon rind and juice, parsley, thyme and breadcrumbs. Season with salt and pepper. Lay the herrings flat out, flesh side up. Spread some stuffing over each herring, then roll up from heat to tail. Secure them by pressing the small piece of tailbone remaining into the flesh.

Place the herrings in a buttered ovenproof dish, cover with foil and bake until the flesh feels firm — about 35 mins. Serve hot, garnished with mushrooms, parsley and lemon wedges.

serves 4
working time 45 mins
total time 1 hour 25 mins

calories 530
total fat 40 g
saturated fat 9 g

cod stewed with onions, potatoes, sweetcorn and tomatoes

1 tbsp virgin olive oil

500 g (1 lb) onions, thinly sliced

1 kg (2 lb) potatoes, peeled and thinly sliced

500 g (1 lb) fresh or frozen sweetcorn

1/2 green pepper, seeded and diced

Tabasco

500 g (1 lb) cod or haddock, skinned and cut into chunks

1.25 kg (2^1/2 lb) tomatoes, skinned, seeded and chopped, or 800 g (28 oz) canned tomatoes, chopped and drained

1/4 tsp salt

freshly ground black pepper

fresh coriander leaves for garnish (optional)

In a large pan, heat the oil over a medium heat. Add a layer of onions and a layer of potatoes. Sprinkle some of the sweetcorn and green peppers on top. Dribble a few drops of Tabasco over the vegetables. Add a layer of fish and tomatoes and season with all of the salt and some pepper.

Repeat, building up successive layers until all the vegetables and fish are used. Cover the pan and cook over a medium-low heat until the potatoes are done – about 45 minutes.

Garnish the stew with coriander leaves. Serve at once.

serves
working time 15 mins
total time 1 hour

calories 310
total fat 4 g
saturated fat 1 g

hints and tips

It is good to have plenty of fresh crusty bread to mop up the end of the stew!

baked coley, tomatoes
and courgettes

500 g (1 lb) coley fillets (or cod or
haddock)
1/4 tsp salt
freshly ground black pepper
1 tbsp virgin olive oil
2 tbsp chopped fresh basil
2 garlic cloves, finely chopped
750 g (1 1/2 lb) tomatoes, skinned,
seeded and chopped, or 400 g
(14 oz) canned tomatoes, chopped
and drained
1 small courgette, sliced diagonally
into thin ovals
60 g (2 oz) hard smoked cheese, cut
into thin narrow strips

Preheat the oven to 200°C (400°F or Mark 6). Rinse the fillets under cold water, and pat dry. Sprinkle $1/8$ tsp of the salt and some pepper over both sides of the fillets. Spread the oil on the bottom of an ovenproof casserole. Arrange the fillets in the dish in a single layer.

Strew the basil and garlic over the fish, then cover with the tomatoes. Arrange the courgette slices in a fish scale pattern down the centre of the dish. Sprinkle the remaining salt over them. Cover fish with a piece of oiled greaseproof paper and bake it for 10 minutes. Remove the paper and place the strips of cheese in a diamond pattern around the courgette. Cover the dish again and bake until the fish is firm to the touch – 3 to 5 minutes more. Serve immediately.

serves 4
working time 15 mins
total time 30 mins

calories 215
total fat 9 g
saturated fat 3 g

French bread with hot prawn and garlic filling

90 g (3 oz) medium-fat curd cheese
$1/2$ garlic clove, crushed
2 tsp finely chopped parsley, chives and dill
1 tsp fresh lemon juice
freshly ground black pepper
175 g (6 oz) cooked peeled prawns, chopped
1 baguette, about 60 cm (2 feet) long, or 6 crusty rolls

Preheat the oven to 220°C (425°F or Mark 7). In a medium-sized bowl, mix together the cheese, garlic, herbs, lemon juice and some freshly ground black pepper. Stir in the prawns.

Cut deep diagonal slashes at 4 cm ($1^1/2$ inch) intervals in the baguette, taking care not to slice right through. Stuff the slashes with the prawn mixture. Wrap the baguette loosely in foil and bake in the oven for 10 minutes. Serve hot.

serves 6
working time 10 mins
total time 20 mins

calories 165
total fat 5 g
saturated fat trace

ULTIMATE
budget cookbook

anchovy toasts

4 thin slices bread
45 g (1¹/₂ oz) small anchovy fillets,
rinsed and drained
60 g (2 oz) margarine
¹/₂ tsp fresh lemon juice
¹/₈ tsp cayenne pepper
freshly ground black pepper
parsley or lemon wedges for garnish

Preheat the oven to 180°C (355°F or Mark 4). Cut out a diamond-shaped piece of cardboard, with sides 5 cm (2 inch) long. Use this template to cut 16 diamonds from the bread. Place the diamonds on a baking sheet and bake until golden on both sides – about 25 minutes. Set aside.

Reserve 4 whole anchovy fillets and pound the rest in a mortar until a smooth paste is obtained. Gradually beat in the margarine and season with the lemon juice, cayenne pepper and some freshly ground black pepper.

Spread the anchovy mixture evenly onto the toasts, then draw the tines of a fork through the mixture to produce decorative lines. Cut each of the reserved anchovies into 4 long, thin strips. Twist each strip and lay it on top of a toast. Serve garnished, if you like, with parsley or lemon wedges.

makes 16 toasts
working time about 15 mins
total time about 40 mins

calories 50
total fat 4 g
saturated fat 1 g

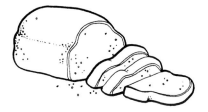

seafood chilli with peppers

185 g (6$^1/_2$ oz) dried black beans, soaked and cooked
500 g (1 lb) mixed seafood
1 lime, sliced into thin rounds
1$^1/_4$ tsp ground cumin
$^1/_8$ tsp ground ginger
3$^1/_4$ tsp chilli powder
3 tbsp fresh coriander, chopped
2 garlic cloves, finely chopped
$^1/_2$ green chilli pepper, chopped
3 tbsp safflower oil
1 onion, cut into chunks
$^1/_2$ tsp dried tarragon
$^1/_4$ tsp salt
$^1/_4$ tsp ground cloves
$^1/_4$ tsp ground cinnamon
$^1/_8$ tsp cayenne pepper
350 ml (12 fl oz) chicken stock
400 g (14 oz) canned chopped tomatoes

10 small green tomatoes
1 sweet red pepper, seeded, cut into chunks
1 sweet yellow pepper, seeded, cut into chunks

Combine the mixed fish with $^1/_4$ tsp of cumin, the ginger, $^1/_4$ tsp chilli powder, $^1/_4$ tbsp coriander, half the garlic, the chilli pepper and 1 tbsp of the oil in a large bowl. Marinate for 30 minutes.

Meanwhile, heat the remaining oil and sauté the green tomatoes and peppers for 2 minutes. Add the onion and remaining garlic and cook until the onion is translucent – about 5 minutes. Add the remaining spices and cook for 2 to 3 minutes. Add the stock and tomatoes. Bring to the boil, then cover, and simmer until thickened. Add the beans and set aside.

Spread the cooked vegetables over the chilli base and simmer. Lay the marinated seafood on top of the vegetables, cover and steam until the fish is opaque. Serve with a coriander garnish.

serves 4
working time 1 hour 30 mins
total time 3 hours 30 mins

calories 450
total fat 14 g
saturated fat 1 g

fish and tomato gratin

30 g (1 oz) plaice fillets, skinned
350 g (12 oz) tomatoes, skinned, seeded and chopped
1 garlic clove, crushed
1 tbsp chopped fresh basil
1 tsp tomato purée
freshly ground black pepper
6 tbsp fromage frais
2 tbsp fresh lemon juice
2 egg whites
3 tbsp fresh white breadcrumbs

Preheat the oven to 190°C (375°F or Mark 5). Bring some water to the boil in a large pan. Poach the white fish for 2 to 3 minutes. Drain the fillets and set them aside.

Mix together the tomatoes, garlic, basil, tomato purée and some pepper. Divide among 4 individual gratin dishes.

Using a fork, flake the cooked fish and place it in a bowl with the fromage frais and lemon juice. Whisk the egg whites in another bowl until stiff. Fold them into the fish mixture. Season with more freshly ground black pepper.

Spoon the fish mixture over the tomato and sprinkle the breadcrumbs over the fish. Bake the gratins until the filling is heated through and the breadcrumbs are crisp – 25 to 30 minutes. Serve the gratins hot.

serves 4
working time 25 mins
total time 55 mins

calories 135
total fat 4 g
saturated fat 1 g

hints and tips

If you can't get plaice at the fishmongers then substitute with any available white fish.

These are probably the most economical ingredients you can buy — and the fastest to cook. What's more, virtually all the supermarkets sell bumper, family-sized bags of pasta — so as long as your family aren't too fussed over whether they're eating bows, tubes or ribbons, it's always possible to take advantage of special promotions. Pasta in particular is also so versatile as it can be used as the basis for quick suppers as well as dinner party specials. And any leftovers can either be reused or pressed into service by being transformed into an enticing salad or side dish. The other advantage of these ingredients is that as they're non-perishable (they won't go off) which means that the packets can be left quite happily in the cupboard until you need something quick— or you just fancy a treat! Beans can also form the basis of an inexpensive meal but compare prices of canned and dried beans as dried can often end up much cheaper. You just need to remember that the dried version needs to be soaked — often the easiest way is to soak them overnight — so you need to plan ahead.

hot chickpea salad

350 g (12 oz) chickpeas
6 tbsp finely chopped flat-leaf parsley
2 tbsp finely chopped fresh oregano
1 onion, finely chopped
virgin olive oil
red wine vinegar
salt
freshly ground black pepper

Rinse the chickpeas under cold water, then put in a large pan, and pour in enough cold water to cover them by about 7.5 cm (3 inches). Discard any that float to the surface. Cover the pan, leaving the lid ajar, and slowly bring to the boil, over medium-low heat. Boil the chickpeas for 2 minutes, then turn off the heat and soak for at least one hour. Drain the peas, return them to the pan and cover with at least twice their volume of fresh water. Bring to the boil, reduce the heat to maintain a simmer, and cook the peas until they are tender – about 1 hour.

Meanwhile, combine the parsley and oregano in a small bowl, and put the chopped onion in a second bowl. When the chickpeas are cooked, drain them in a colander and transfer them to a warm serving dish. Serve immediately, accompanied by cruets of oil and vinegar, the bowls of chopped herbs and onion, and the seasonings. The salad can be dressed individually to taste.

serves 6
working time 20 mins
total time 2 hours 10 mins
(inc soaking)

calories 240
total fat 8 g   saturated fat 1 g

hints and tips

Why not try a different vinegar as a dressing, for example, balsamic.

chickpea and burghul kofta

250 g (8 oz) dried chickpeas
125 g (4 oz) burghul, soaked for
30 mins, drained and squeezed dry
2 tbsp tahini
6 tbsp plain low-fat yoghurt
1 small onion, grated
1 garlic clove, crushed
4 tbsp chopped parsley
4 tbsp chopped mint
1 lemon, juice only
lettuce leaves
lemon wedges

chilli tomato relish:
1 tbsp virgin olive oil
500 g (1 lb) tomatoes, chopped
1 small onion, finely chopped
1 cucumber, finely chopped
2 or 3 fresh hot chilli peppers,
seeded and finely chopped

Rinse the chickpeas then transfer them to a large pan and pour in enough water to cover them by about 7.5 cm (3 inches). Discard any chickpeas that float to the surface. Cover the pan, leaving the lid ajar, and bring to the boil. Boil for 2 minutes, then turn off the heat. Cover the pan and soak the peas for at least one hour.

Drain and rinse the chickpeas, return them to the pan and pour in enough water to cover them by 7.5 cm (3 inches). Bring to the boil, then reduce the heat to maintain a simmer and cook the peas, covered, until they are soft – about $1^1/_4$ hours – adding more hot water if required.

Drain the chickpeas, then purée them in a blender. Stir in the burghul, tahini, yoghurt, onion, garlic, parsley, mint and lemon juice. Form the mixture into 16 boat shapes, chill them for 1 hour.

Meanwhile, begin to make the relish. Heat the oil in a pan over low heat. Add the tomatoes and cook them gently, covered, for 15 minutes. Sieve the tomatoes and chill the purée for 1 hour.

Preheat the grill to high and cover a grill rack with foil. Grill the kofta until golden-brown – 3 to 4 minutes on each side. Meanwhile, stir in the onion, cucumber and chillies into the tomato purée. Serve the kofta hot, garnished with the lettuce leaves and lemon wedges.

serves 4
working time 45 mins
total time 4 hours
(inc soaking and chilling)

calories 430
total fat 12 g   saturated fat 2 g

hints and tips

If you don't have time to prepare the relish, check out the fresh relishes and dips from the supermarket or delicatessen.

pea and mushroom risotto

350 g (12 oz) peas, shelled, or
125 g (4 oz) frozen peas, thawed
30 g (1 oz) unsalted butter
125 g (4 oz) shallots, chopped
500 g (1 lb) brown rice
200 ml (7 fl oz) dry white wine or
dry vermouth
450 ml ($3/4$ pint) tomato juice
450 ml ($3/4$ pint) vegetable stock
250 g (8 oz) tomatoes, skinned,
seeded and chopped
$1/2$ tsp salt
250 g (8 oz) chestnut mushrooms,
wiped and grated
60 g (2 oz) Parmesan cheese, grated
freshly ground black pepper
chopped parsley, for garnish

If you are using fresh peas, boil until barely tender – 3 to 4 minutes. Drain them, then refresh them under cold running water. Drain them again and set aside (frozen peas do not need precooking).

In a large pan, melt the butter and sauté the shallots over medium heat until they are transparent, stirring occasionally – 3 to 5 minutes. Stir the rice into the shallots and cook for 2 to 3 minutes, stirring constantly, to make sure the grains are well coated with the butter.

Pour the wine into the rice and simmer, stirring frequently until the wine has been absorbed. Pour in the tomato juice and add 300 ml ($1/2$ pint) of the stock. Bring to the boil then reduce the heat to a simmer. Cover the pan and cook the rice, stirring occasionally, for about 20 minutes. Stir the tomatoes and the salt into the rice. Cover and simmer for a further 10 minutes, adding more stock, a ladleful at a time if the rice dries out. Add the mushrooms, peas, and any remaining stock to the pan. Increase the heat and cook rapidly, stirring constantly until the stock is absorbed but the rice is still very moist. Stir the Parmesan cheese into the risotto and season generously with freshly ground black pepper. Turn the risotto into a warmed serving dish and sprinkle with chopped parsley.

serves 6
working time 45 mins
total time 1 hour 15 mins

calories 410
total fat 10 g
saturated fat 5 g

hints and tips

It's always wise to have some frozen vegetables in the freezer. Frozen vegetables retain the vitamins, minerals and taste of fresh vegetables.

ULTIMATE
budget cookbook

risotto with carrots and coriander

45 g (1^1/$_2$ oz) unsalted butter
1 onion, finely chopped
1 litre (1^1/$_4$ pints) chicken stock
2 tsp ground coriander
300 g (10 oz) carrots, finely diced
350 g (12 oz) Italian
round-grain rice
freshly ground black pepper
45 g (1^1/$_2$ oz) Parmesan, grated
1 small bunch fresh coriander
leaves, finely chopped

In a large pan, heat 30 g (1 oz) of the butter and sauté the onion until it is transparent – 3 to 5 minutes. Meanwhile, bring the stock to the boil in a pan. Stir in the coriander, reduce the heat and keep the liquid simmering gently.

Add the diced carrots to the onion and sauté for about 5 minutes. Add the ice and stir well, to ensure the grains are coated with butter. Ladle a few spoonfuls of the hot stock into the rice and stir well, and let the mixture cook, stirring occasionally until most of the liquid has been absorbed. Continue adding hot stock, a little at a time, stirring constantly and replenishing the liquid as the rice absorbs it. cook the rice until it is moist but not swimming in stock and the grains have lost their brittleness but still have a chewy core – about 20 minutes. Remove the rice from the heat and add the remaining butter, Parmesan and some pepper. Stir well, cover the pan and let the risotto stand for 5 minutes. Stir the rice and sprinkle with the coriander before serving.

serves 6
total time 1 hour

calories 300
total fat 11 g
saturated fat 6 g

linguine with broad beans and grainy mustard

250 g (8 oz) linguine
250 g (8 oz) ripe plum tomatoes
175 ml (6 fl oz) chicken stock
165 g (5^1/$_2$ oz) fresh or frozen broad beans
^{1}/$_4$ tsp salt
2 spring onions, thinly sliced
1^1/$_2$ tbsp grainy mustard
30 g (1 oz) unsalted butter

Place a tomato on a cutting surface with its stem end down. With a small sharp knife, cut wide strips of flesh from the tomato, discarding the seeds and juice. Slice each piece of tomato flesh into 5 mm (^{1}/$_4$ inch) wide strips and set them aside. Repeat with the remaining tomatoes.

Pour the stock into a frying pan over medium heat, and bring it to a simmer. Add the beans and salt and cook for 6 minutes. Stir in the spring onions and mustard. Simmer for one minute more. Add the butter and tomato strips then simmer for an additional 2 minutes, stirring once.

Meanwhile cook the linguine in boiling water, with 1^1/$_2$ tsp salt. Start testing the pasta after 10 minutes and cook until it is al dente. Drain the linguine and transfer it to the pan with the bean mixture. Toss well to coat the pasta and serve immediately.

serves 4
total time 20 mins

calories 345
total fat 8 g
saturated fat 4 g

hints and tips

You can use spaghetti or any other long pasta instead of linguine.

ULTIMATE
budget cookbook

provencal casserole

250 g (8 oz) dried flageolet beans

1 tbsp virgin olive oil

1 large onion, sliced

1 garlic clove, crushed

1 sweet red pepper, seeded and sliced

500 g (1 lb) courgettes, thickly sliced

1 aubergine, cut into large dice

500 g (1 lb) tomatoes, skinned, seeded and chopped, or 300 g (10 oz) canned tomatoes, chopped and drained

125 g (4 oz) button mushrooms, stems trimmed

150 ml ($^{1}/_{4}$ pint) vegetable stock

2 tsp chopped fresh oregano

$^{1}/_{4}$ tsp freshly ground black pepper

$^{1}/_{4}$ tsp salt

Rinse the beans under cold water and put into a large pan. Pour in enough cold water to cover them by about 7.5 cm (3 inches). Discard any beans that float to the top. Bring the water to the boil and cook the beans for 2 minutes. Turn off the heat, partially cover the pan and soak the beans for at least one hour.

Rinse the beans, place in a clean pan and pour in enough water to cover them by about 7.5 cm (3 inches). Bring to the boil. Boil the beans for 10 minutes then drain and rinse them again. Wash out the pan. Replace the beans. Cover them again by 7.5 cm (3 inches) of water and bring to the boil. Reduce the heat to maintain a strong simmer and cook the beans, covered, until they are tender – about 1 hour. If the beans are drying out at any point, pour in more hot water. When they are cooked, drain and rinse the beans in a colander.

Heat the oil in a large casserole and cook the onion and garlic over a low heat for a few mins until softened but not browned. Add the red pepper, courgettes, aubergine and tomatoes, and cook over low heat for 1 to 2 minutes, stirring frequently.

Reduce the heat and add the mushrooms, beans, stock, oregano, freshly ground black pepper and salt. Mix well, cover and simmer over low heat, stirring occasionally for 25 minutes or until the vegetables are tender. Serve hot.

serves 6
working time 30 mins
total time 3 hours (inc soaking)

calories 180
total fat 3 g
saturated fat 1 g

vegetable lasagne

1 tbsp virgin olive oil
1 onion, chopped
1 leek, thinly sliced
2 garlic cloves, crushed
175 g (6 oz) broccoli florets
125 g (4 oz) French beans, cut into
2.5 cm (1 inch) lengths
6 sticks celery, thinly sliced
1 small yellow pepper, seeded and
thinly sliced
1 tsp mixed dried herbs
1 tbsp chopped parsley
400 g (14 oz) canned tomatoes,
sieved
$1/4$ tsp salt
freshly ground black pepper
30 g (1 oz) Parmesan, grated

spinach pasta dough:
175 g (6 oz) strong plain flour
250 g (8 oz) fresh spinach, blanched for 1 minute in boiling water, finely
chopped or 150 g (5 oz) frozen chopped spinach, thawed
1 egg white
1 tbsp safflower oil

nutmeg sauce:
30 g (1 oz) butter
30 g (1 oz) plain flour
300 ml ($1/2$ pint) skimmed milk
$1/2$ tsp freshly grated nutmeg
$1/8$ tsp salt
freshly ground black pepper

Heat the oil in a large pan over medium heat. Add the onion and leek and cook for 6 to 8 minutes, until softened. Stir in the garlic, all of the vegetables and herbs, the tomatoes, salt and some pepper. Bring to the boil, then reduce the heat and partially cover the pan with a lid. Cook gently for 45 minutes, until the vegetables are tender and the liquid has thickened.

Meanwhile, make the pasta. Put the flour into a bowl and make a well in the centre. Add the spinach, egg white and oil and stir them, using a fork or wooden spoon, gradually incorporating the flour. Transfer the dough to a floured surface and knead for a few mins. The dough should come cleanly away from the surface. If it is too wet, add flour by the tablespoon until the dough is no longer sticky. If the dough is too dry, add water by the teaspoon until it is pliable. Continue kneading until it is smooth and elastic – about 10 minutes.

serves 6
working time 1 hour 30 mins
total time 2 hours 15 mins

calories 295
total fat 12 g
saturated fat 5 g

Wrap the dough in greaseproof paper or Clingfilm and let it rest for 15 minutes.

Roll out the dough in a floured surface into a rectangle about 60 x 45 cm (24 x 18 inches). It should be about 1 mm ($^{1}/_{16}$ inch) thick. Cut the rectangle lengthwise into three strips, then cut each of these crosswise into 6 pieces, to make a total of 18 sheets of lasagne.

Preheat the oven to 200°C (400°F or Mark 6).

Cook the lasagne for 1 minute, three or four sheets at a time, in 3 litres (5 pints) boiling water. Lift the sheets out with a slotted spoon and spread them on a clean towel to drain.

Grease a 25 x 20 x 5cm (10 x 8 x 2 inch) ovenproof dish and line the bottom with 6 sheets of lasagne. Pour in half the vegetable filling and cover it with another six sheets of lasagne. Pour in the rest of the vegetables and arrange the remaining lasagne sheets over the top.

To make the sauce, melt the butter in a pan over medium heat. Add the flour, then gradually stir in the milk. Bring to the boil, stirring continuously, until it thickens. Stir in the nutmeg, salt and some pepper. Reduce the heat to low and simmer for 5 minutes, stirring frequently. Pour the sauce over the top of the lasagne and spread it to cover the entire surface. Sprinkle the Parmesan evenly over the sauce. Cook the lasagne in the oven for 40 minutes, until golden-brown and bubbling hot.

black bean, rice and pepper salad

185 g (2 oz) black beans, soaked for
8 hours or overnight

1 small onion, chopped

1 garlic clove

2 tsp fresh thyme or $^1/_2$ tsp dried
thyme

1 bay leaf

$^1/_2$ tsp salt

1 litre ($1^3/_4$ pints) chicken stock

370 g (13 oz) long-grain rice

2 shallots, finely chopped

1 sweet red pepper, seeded and
sliced into thin, short strips

1 hot green chilli pepper, seeded
and finely chopped

3 spring onions, trimmed and thinly
sliced

2 tbsp chopped fresh coriander or
parsley

chilli dressing:

1 tsp Dijon mustard

1 tbsp white wine vinegar

1 tbsp chicken stock

2 tbsp virgin olive oil

$^1/_2$ tsp chilli powder

4 drops Tabasco

1 garlic clove, finely chopped

freshly ground black pepper

Put the beans into a large pan, pour in enough cold water to cover them by about 7.5 cm (3 inches). Bring water to the boil. Boil for 10 minutes then drain. Return to the pan, add enough water to cover them by 7.5 cm (3 inches). Bring to the boil. Add the onion, garlic, thyme and bay leaf to the beans. Cover the pan and simmer for 50 minutes, until they are soft, occasionally skimming foam from the surface. Stir in the salt and continue cooking until the beans are quite tender – 30 minutes to one hour more. If the beans appear to be drying out, pour in more water. Transfer the beans to a colander. Remove the garlic clove and bay leaf then rinse the beans and drain well.

Bring the stock to the boil in a small pan. Add the rice and shallots, and lower the heat to maintain a simmer. Cook the rice, covered, until it is tender and liquid is absorbed – about 20 minutes.

While the rice is cooking, prepare the dressing. Combine the mustard, vinegar and the tablespoon of stock in a small bowl. Whisk in the oil, then the chilli powder, Tabasco, garlic and some pepper.

Transfer the rice to a large bowl, add the peppers, spring onions and beans. Pour the dressing over the salad. Toss well and chill for at least one hour. Sprinkle with coriander and parsley before serving.

serves 4
working time 20 mins
total time 11 hours
(inc soaking and chilling)

calories 635
total fat 10 g   saturated fat 1 g

ULTIMATE
budget cookbook

spirals with liver, onions and peas

250 g (8 oz) spirals, or other short pasta

2 tbsp virgin olive oil

125 g (4 oz) chicken livers, cut into 1 cm ($1/2$ inch) pieces

$1/4$ tsp salt

2 onions, thinly sliced

4 tbsp cider vinegar

15 g ($1/2$ oz) butter

250 g (8 oz) mange-tout or peas

freshly ground black pepper

Heat 1 tbsp of oil in a large frying pan, over medium-high heat. Sauté the chicken liver pieces, stirring, until brown – 30 to 45 seconds. Sprinkle the liver with $1/8$ tsp of salt. Remove from pan and set aside.

Return the pan to the heat without washing it, and add the remaining tablespoon of oil. Add the onions and vinegar, and stir to deglaze the pan. Cook, stirring frequently, until the onions are golden brown – about 15 minutes. Meanwhile, cook the pasta in water. Begin testing the pasta after 8 minutes, and cook until it is al dente.

While the pasta is cooking, melt the butter in a frying pan over medium heat. Add the peas and cook them until tender – about 7 minutes. Sprinkle the peas with the salt and some pepper. Drain the pasta and add it to the pan of onions. Add the reserved liver and peas. Toss thoroughly and serve immediately.

serves 4
total time 35 mins

calories 375
total fat 12 g
saturated fat 3 g

hints and tips

There are so many different pastas available, try others and don't stick to just one or two.

penne with mushrooms and tarragon

250 g (8 oz) penne, or other short
pasta
15 g ($^1/_2$ oz) dried ceps or porcini
mushrooms
2 tbsp virgin olive oil
1 small onion, finely chopped
250 g (8 oz) button mushrooms, cut
into 5 mm ($^1/_4$ inch) dice
$^1/_2$ tsp salt
freshly ground black pepper
3 garlic cloves, finely chopped
$^1/_4$ litre (8 fl oz) dry white wine
750 g (1$^1/_2$ lb) tomatoes, skinned,
seeded and chopped
6tbsp chopped parsley
2 tbsp chopped fresh tarragon

Pour $^1/_4$ litre (8 fl oz) hot water over the mushrooms and soak them until they are soft – about 20 minutes. Drain the ceps and reserve their soaking liquid. Cut into 5 mm ($^1/_4$ inch) pieces. Heat the oil in a frying pan over medium heat. Add the onion and sauté it until translucent – about 4 minutes. Add the ceps, button mushrooms, salt and pepper. Cook until the mushrooms begin to brown – 5 minutes. Add the garlic and wine and cook the mixture until the liquid is reduced to approximately 2 tbsp – about 5 minutes more.

Add the penne to water and boil. Start testing the pasta after 10 minutes and continue to cook until it is al dente.

When the penne is cooking, pour the reserved cep-soaking liquid into the pan of mushrooms, and cook until the liquid is reduced to approximately 4 tbsp – about 5 minutes. Stir in the tomatoes and cook until it is heated through – 3 minutes more. Drain the pasta and add to the pan, with the chopped parsley and tarragon. Toss well and serve.

serves 4
total time 45 mins

calories 385
total fat 8 g
saturated fat 1 g

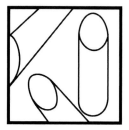

ULTIMATE
budget cookbook

sweet and sour cabbage cannelloni

12 cannelloni
30 g (1 oz) butter
1 small onion, finely chopped
500 g (1 lb) green cabbage, shredded
1 carrot, peeled and grated
1 apple, peeled, cored and grated
$1/4$ tsp salt
1.25 kg ($2^1/2$ lb) ripe tomatoes, quartered
1 tbsp dark brown sugar
2 tbsp white wine vinegar
4 tbsp raisins

To prepare the cabbage stuffing, melt the butter in a large frying pan over medium heat. Add the onion and sauté it until it turns translucent – about 4 minutes. Pour 5 mm ($1/4$ inch) of water in a pan. Stir in the cabbage, carrot, apple and $1/8$ tsp of salt. Cover the pan and steam the vegetables, adding more water as necessary, until they are soft – 30 minutes. Set the pan aside. Meanwhile, pour 4 tbsp of water into a pan over medium-high heat. Add tomatoes and cook them, stirring frequently, until soft – about 20 minutes. Transfer the tomatoes to a sieve and allow the liquid to drain off. Discard the liquid and purée the tomatoes into a bowl. Stir in the brown sugar, vinegar, raisins and the remaining salt. To prepare the cannelloni, add to boiling water with 2 tbsp salt. Start testing the cannelloni after 15 minutes. Cook until they are al dente. With a slotted spoon, transfer the tubes to a large bowl of cold water.

Preheat the oven to 200°C (400°F or Mark 6). Drain the cannelloni and fill each one carefully with $1/12$ of the cabbage stuffing. Arrange the tubes in a single layer in a baking dish. Pour the stock over them, then cover the dish with foil. Bake for 30 minutes. 10 minutes before serving, transfer the sauce to a pan and bring it to the boil. Reduce the heat to low and simmer gently while the cannelloni finish cooking. Serve immediately; pass the sauce separately.

serves 6
working time 45 mins
total time 1 hour 30 mins

calories 295
total fat 6 g
saturated fat 3 g

hints and tips

Try some other varieties of cabbage if green cabbages are not available.

egg noodles with poppy seeds, yoghurt and mushrooms

250 g (8 oz) medium egg noodles
4 tbsp soured cream
125 ml (4 fl oz) low-fat yoghurt
1 tbsp poppy seeds
$1/8$ to $1/4$ tsp cayenne pepper
2 tbsp virgin olive oil
250 g (8 oz) mushrooms, thinly sliced
1 onion, chopped
$1/4$ tsp salt
125 ml (4 fl oz) dry white wine

In a small bowl, combine the sour cream, yoghurt, poppy seeds, cayenne pepper and 1 tbsp of the oil. In a large covered pan, cook the egg noodles in boiling water until al dente – about 9 minutes.

While the noodles are cooking, heat the remaining oil in a frying pan, over medium-high heat. Add the mushrooms and onion, and sprinkle with the $1/4$ tsp of salt. Cook, stirring frequently, until the mushrooms and onion are browned all over – 5 to 7 minutes. Add the wine to the pan, and continue cooking, stirring, until almost all the liquid has been absorbed – about 3 minutes more. When the noodles are done, drain them and add to the pan. Add the yoghurt and poppy seed mixture, toss well and serve.

serves 8
total time 25 mins

calories 195
total fat 6 g
saturated fat 2 g

ULTIMATE
budget cookbook

vermicelli, onions and peas

250 g (8 oz) vermicelli or
spaghettini
2 tbsp virgin olive oil
500 g (1 lb) onions, chopped
1 leek, thinly sliced
$1/4$ tsp salt
freshly ground black pepper
$1/4$ litre (8 fl oz) dry white wine
75 g ($2^1/_2$ oz) shelled peas

Heat in the oil in a large frying pan over low heat. Add the onions, leek, salt and freshly ground black pepper, cover the pan and cook, stirring to keep the onions from sticking, until the vegetables are soft – about 35 minutes.

Cook the pasta in boiling water. Test the pasta after 7 minutes and cook until it is al dente.

While the pasta is cooking, finish the sauce. Pour the wine into the pan and raise the heat to high. Cook the mixture until the liquid is reduced to about 4 tbsp – approximately 5 minutes. Stir in the peas, cover the pan and cook for another 1 to 2 minutes to heat the peas through. If using fresh peas, cook for 5 minutes.

Drain the pasta and transfer to a serving dish. Pour the contents of the frying pan over the top. Toss well and serve immediately.

serves 8
working time 15 mins
total time 1 hour

calories 185
total fat 4 g
saturated fat 1 g

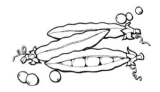

grated pasta with green beans and cheddar

200 g (6 oz) strong plain flour

1 egg

1 egg white

$^1/_2$ tsp salt

125 g (4 oz) green beans, stemmed, thinly sliced diagonally

$^1/_2$ litre (16 fl oz)

$^1/_4$ tsp white pepper

$^1/_8$ tsp cayenne pepper

90 g (3 oz) grated cheddar cheese

4 tbsp fresh breadcrumbs

Pour the flour in a mixing bowl and form a well in the middle. Briefly beat the egg white and $^1/_4$ tsp of the salt in another bowl. Then pour the beaten egg into the flour. Mix with a large spoon until the flour begins to form clumps. Add enough cold water – 1 to 2 tbsp – to allow you to form the mixture into a ball with your hands. Work the last of the flour into the dough by hand, then turn the dough out onto a flour-dusted surface and knead it until it is firm and smooth – about 5 minutes. Wrap the dough in plastic film and freeze it for at least $1^1/_2$ hours.

Remove the dough, unwrap it and grate it on the coarse side of a hand grater. Blanch the beans in boiling water for 2 minutes, then refresh them under cold water. Preheat oven to 180°C (355°F or Mark 4).

Bring the milk to a simmer over low heat in a large pan. Add the grated noodles, white pepper, cayenne pepper and the remaining $^1/_4$ tsp of salt. Simmer the mixture, stirring occasionally until the noodles have absorbed almost all of the liquid – 4 to 5 minutes. Add the green beans and half of the grated cheese. Stir thoroughly.

Transfer the contents of the pan to a casserole. Combine the remaining cheese with the breadcrumbs and sprinkle the mixture over the top. Bake until the crust is crisp and golden – about 20 minutes – and serve hot.

serves 6
working time 20 mins
total time 1 hour 20 mins

calories 230
total fat 6 g
saturated fat 4 g

ULTIMATE
budget cookbook

pasta with fresh herbs and garlic

400 g (14 oz) fusilli
250 g (8 oz) fromage frais
2 tbsp chopped parsley
1 tbsp chopped fresh oregano
2 tbsp chopped fresh thyme
1 tbsp chopped fresh mint
2 tbsp virgin olive oil
$1/2$ garlic clove, finely chopped
$1/4$ tsp salt
freshly ground black pepper

Cook the pasta in lightly salted boiling water until it is al dente — about 9 minutes. Meanwhile, in a small bowl, combine the fromage frais, chopped parsley, oregano, thyme and mint with the olive oil and chopped garlic. Season with the salt and some freshly ground black pepper. When the fusilli are cooked, drain in a colander but leave a little of the cooking water clinging to the pasta. This will thin down the herb, cheese and garlic mixture to form a sauce. Stir the herb mixture into the pasta and serve hot.

serves 8
working time 10 mins
total time 20 mins

calories 250
total fat 7 g
saturated fat 1 g

hints and tips

Vary the taste of this dish by introducing other fresh herbs.

Vegetable-based meals are no longer just for the vegetarians! The recipes these days are so tempting and irresistible that you just want to dive in there – irrelevant of whether you're a meat and two veg man – or woman - or a vegan!

Although a vast selection of vegetables are available throughout the year the secret of getting the best out of your veg is to buy what's in season. That way you get something in peak condition, that you know has only recently been picked, and is also likely to be good value. Look out for gluts – if supermarkets are left with large stocks of fresh produce they'll often sell it off at a considerably reduced price at the end of the day as the alternative may be that they'll have to chuck it, as it's likely to go off. Remember, anything not in season is likely to be at a premium.

But that doesn't mean you have to be restricted in terms of what you make. There are quite a few recipes where frozen vegetables are fine to use, with the added advantage that the whole process of freezing means that the vegetables retain their nutrients. In fact, some frozen veg are actually likely to contain more vitamins and minerals than fresh fruit and veg that may have been lying around for a while and have clearly seen better days!

spiced red cabbage

1 tbsp juniper berries
1 tbsp coriander seeds
2 tbsp virgin olive oil
5 garlic cloves, sliced
1 large red cabbage, trimmed and sliced
300 ml ($^1/_2$ pint) dry cider
freshly ground black pepper
3 large green cooking apples, cored, peeled, halved and placed in acidulated water

Preheat the oven to 180°C (355°F or Mark 4). Crush the juniper berries and coriander seeds, using a mortar and pestle. Heat the oil over medium heat in a 7 litre (12 pint) casserole. Add the garlic and crushed spices and stir-fry them briefly. Add the red cabbage and fry for 3 to 4 minutes. Remove the casserole from the heat, pour the cider over the cabbage and season with black pepper. Cover the casserole and cook the cabbage in the oven for 1 hour.

Stir in the cabbage and transfer it to a $3^1/_2$ litre (6 pint) casserole. The cabbage will have halved in volume by this stage. Drain the apple halves, and pat dry. Lay them on top of the cabbage. Cover the casserole and return the cabbage to the oven for a further 30 minutes.

Preheat the grill to medium. Remove the casserole from the oven. Take off the lid and, without stirring the contents, lay the slices of cheese over the apples. Put the casserole under the grill for about 5 minutes, until the cheese has melted and begun to brown. Serve at once.

serves 6
working time 20 mins
total time 1 hour 50 mins

calories 330
total fat 13 g
saturated fat 4 g

ULTIMATE
budget cookbook

herbed vegetable brochettes

2 small courgettes, trimmed and cut into 1 cm (1/2 inch) rounds
12 small button mushrooms
12 baby sweetcorn cobs, cut into 2 or 3 pieces
1/2 sweet pepper, cut into 12 squares
12 cherry tomatoes
6 lime wedges

herb marinade:
4 tbsp virgin olive oil
2 tbsp fresh lemon juice
1/2 tsp grated lemon rind
1 garlic clove, crushed
1 tsp Dijon mustard
3 tbsp chopped mixed fresh herbs

In a bowl, whisk together the marinade ingredients and blend them thoroughly. Add the vegetables to the marinade, coating evenly. Cover the bowl with plastic film and set aside for at least 6 hours, stirring the vegetables occasionally. 20 minutes before cooking the brochettes soak 12 bamboo skewers in water – this keeps them moist and prevents them from burning under the grill.

Preheat the grill. With a slotted spoon, remove the vegetables from the bowl, reserving the marinade. Thread a selection of vegetables onto each skewer. Grill the brochettes about 10 cm (4 inches) from the source of heat, turning occasionally until the vegetables begin to brown – about 10 minutes. Serve the brochettes hot, with the marinade spooned over them. Garnish with lime wedges.

serves 6
working time 25 mins
total time 6 hours 30 mins
(inc marinating)

calories 115
total fat 10 g   saturated fat 2 g

hints and tips

The brochettes are very tasty with a variety of marinades, look out for fresh ones in the supermarket if time is short.

potato, carrot and celeriac rosti

500 g (1 lb) potatoes, scrubbed
250 g (8 oz) carrots, peeled
300 g (10 oz) celeriac, peeled
$1/4$ tsp salt
freshly ground black pepper
45 g ($1^1/2$ oz) butter

Cook the potatoes in their skins in a pan of boiling water for 6 minutes, then drain. Peel the potatoes whilst still hot. Allow to cool for 10 minutes, then chill them for 20 minutes.

Using a vegetable grater or a mouli julienne machine, coarsely shred the potatoes, carrot and celeriac. Place the shredded vegetables in a large bowl. Season with salt and pepper to taste. Mix them well together.

Heat half of the butter in a large frying pan, until it begins to bubble. Reduce the heat to low and add the rosti mixture, pressing it down gently with a spatula, to form a flat cake. Cook for about 10 minutes, until the rosti is golden brown, shaking the pan gently now and then, to prevent sticking.

Place a large flat plate on top of the frying pan. Remove it from the heat and carefully invert the rosti on the plate. Return the pan to the heat, add the remaining butter and heat it until it is bubbling hot. Slide the rosti back into the pan and cook the other side for 5 to 6 minutes until golden brown. Turn the rosti onto a hot plate and serve immediately.

serves 4
working time 40 mins
total time 1 hour 10 mins

calories 200
total fat 9 g
saturated fat 5 g

ULTIMATE
budget cookbook

baked potatoes with onion and chive filling

2 large potatoes, scrubbed and pricked

2 Spanish onions, unpeeled, halved lengthwise

25 g (1 oz) thick Greek yoghurt

2 tbsp finely cut chives

$^1/_2$ tsp salt

freshly ground black pepper

Preheat the oven to 200°C (400°F or Mark 6).

Place the potatoes and onions on a rack in the middle of the onion and bake them until they are soft when pieced with a skewer. The onions will need about 45 minutes and the potatoes about $1^1/_2$ hours. Do not turn off the oven at the end of this time. When the onions are cooked, remove from the oven. Allow them to cool a little, then peel them. Remove and reserve the centres of the onions and roughly chop the remainder.

Cut the cooked potatoes in half lengthwise. Using a spoon, scoop the flesh into a bowl, leaving a 1 cm ($^1/_2$ inch) thick potato shell. Mash the potato flesh, then mix in the yoghurt, chives, salt and pepper.

Half-fill the shells with the mashed potato mixture. Add a layer of chopped roast onion and top this with the rest of the potato mixture. Garnish each potato half with a reserved onion centre. Return the stuffed potatoes to the oven for about 15 minutes to heat them through.

serves 4
working time 20 mins
total time 2 hours

calories 270
total fat 3 g
saturated fat 1 g

hints and tips

Instead of onion and chive, replace the chive with grated cheese to get a cheese and onion filling.

mixed root vegetables cooked in orange sauce

30 g (1 oz) butter
1 onions, chopped
1 garlic clove, crushed
2 tsp freshly grated ginger
1 tsp coriander seeds, crushed
175 g (6 oz) parsnips, peeled, cut into 2.5 cm (1 inch) chunks
175 g (6 oz) carrots, peeled, cut into 2.5 cm (1 inch) chunks
175 g (6 oz) swede, peeled, cut into 2.5 cm (1 inch) chunks
175 g (6 oz) kohlrabi, peeled, cut into 2.5 cm (1 inch) chunks
175 g (6 oz) celeriac, peeled, cut into 2.5 cm (1 inch) chunks
175 g (6 oz) turnips, peeled, cut into 2.5 cm (1 inch) chunks
300 ml (1/2 pint) fresh orange juice, mixed with 150 ml (1/4 pint) water
1 lemon, grated rind only
1 orange, grated rind only
1/2 tsp salt
freshly ground black pepper

serves 4
working time 30 mins
total time 1 hour

calories 160
total fat 7 g
saturated fat 4 g

Melt the butter in a large pan or casserole, over medium heat. Add the onion and garlic and sauté them for 3 to 4 minutes, until the onion is transparent. Mix in the ginger and coriander and cook for a further minute, stirring constantly. Add all the root vegetables and the orange juice and water mixture. Bring to the boil. Reduce the heat to low, cover the pan, and simmer the vegetables for 20 minutes.

Stir in the grated lemon and orange rind, the salt and some freshly ground black pepper. Cover the pan again and simmer the vegetables for another 5 minutes.

Finally, to reduce and thicken the orange sauce, remove the lid from the pan and boil the vegetables rapidly for 5 minutes. At the end of this time, they should feel just tender when pierced with the tip of a small knife.

132

granary pizza with sweetcorn and pineapple

2 tbsp grainy mustard
350 g (12 oz) sweetcorn kernels, fresh or frozen
$^1/_2$ tsp safflower oil
1 large onion, sliced into rings
2 tsp chopped fresh basil, plus basil leaves for garnish
$^1/_8$ tsp paprika
$^1/_2$ small pineapple, skinned and cut into small dice
1 sweet pepper, seeded and cut into 1 cm ($^1/_2$ inch) dice
4 black olives, stoned and quartered
90 g (3 oz) Gouda cheese, grated

pizza dough:
125 g (4 oz) granary flour
125 g (4 oz) plain flour
$^1/_2$ tsp salt
30 g (1 oz) fresh yeast, or 1 tsp dried yeast

serves 4
working time 40 mins
total time 1 hour 45 mins

calories 395
total fat 8 g
saturated fat 4 g

To make the dough for the pizza base, mix both types of flour in a bowl with the salt. In a small bowl, put the fresh yeast in 150 ml ($^1/_4$ pint) warm water. Leave the mixture in a warm place for about 10 minutes until the surface has become frothy. If using dried yeast, activate it according to the manufacturer's instructions. Make a well in the centre of the dry ingredients and pour in the yeast liquid. Using a wooden spoon, mix the ingredients to a soft dough. Turn the dough onto a floured surface and knead it for 5 minutes. Return the dough to the bowl. Cover it with plastic film and leave it in a warm place or about 10 minutes, until it has doubled in size.

Knock back the dough to its original size, then roll it out on a floured surface into a circle about 30 cm (12 inches) in diameter. Place the circle on a greased baking sheet or pizza pan. Brush the dough with mustard, leaving a 1 cm ($^1/_2$ inch) border of dough around the edge. Cover the dough and leave it in a warm place for about 10 minutes, while it rises again. While the dough is rising, preheat the oven to 200°C (400°F or Mark 6) and prepare the filling. Cook the sweetcorn in a pan of simmering water for 3 minutes, then drain them. Heat the oil in a frying pan over medium heat. Add the onion rings and fry them gently for 5 to 6 minutes, until soft. Stir in the basil.

Arrange the onion and basil on the pizza base and sprinkle with paprika. Mix the sweetcorn with pineapple and scatter over the onion. Add the pepper and olives and finally sprinkle with the grated cheese.

Bake the pizza in the oven for 20 to 25 minutes until the dough is crusty around the edges and the cheese has melted. Serve the pizza hot, garnished with shredded basil leaves.

bread, cheese and onion pudding

75 g (2$\frac{1}{2}$ oz) margarine
2 large onions, thinly sliced
500 g (1 lb) courgettes, julienned
2 tsp Dijon mustard
2 garlic cloves, crushed
24 thin slices white bread, crusts removed
2 egg whites
600 ml (1 pint) skimmed milk
freshly ground black pepper
90 g (3 oz) cheddar cheese, grated

Heat 15 g ($\frac{1}{2}$ oz) of the margarine in a large frying pan over medium heat. Add the onions and cook gently for about 5 minutes until they are soft but not brown. Add the courgette juliennes and cook for another 6 minutes, stirring occasionally. Remove the pan from the heat and allow to cool for about 15 minutes.

Put the remaining 60 g (2 oz) of margarine in a small bowl, with the mustard and garlic, and blend them until smooth. Spread the mixture thinly over sliced bread. Cut each slice into four triangles.

Put the eggs, egg whites and milk into a mixing bowl. Add some freshly ground black pepper and whisk the eggs and milk together.

Grease a 30 x 22 cm (12 x 9 inch) ovenproof dish. Place $\frac{1}{3}$ of the bread triangles in a layer in the bottom of the dish and spread half of the onion and courgette mixture over the top. Sprinkle on $\frac{1}{3}$ of the grated cheese. Add another third of the triangles, the remaining onion and courgette mixture and another $\frac{1}{3}$ of the cheese. Arrange the remaining triangles decoratively on the top, overlapping them slightly. Pour the whisked eggs and milk over the bread. Scatter the remaining cheese evenly over the top. Set the pudding aside in a cool place for 1 hour to allow the bread to soften and soak up the eggs and milk.

Preheat the oven to 190° C (375° F or Mark 5). Cook the pudding for 45 to 50 minutes, until it is well puffed up, set and golden brown. Serve immediately.

serves 8
working time 40 mins
total time 2 hours 30 mins

calories 300
total fat 14 g
saturated fat 4 g

mushroom strudel

2 tsp virgin olive oil
1 large onion, chopped
2 garlic cloves, crushed
500 g (1 lb) open mushrooms, finely chopped
2 tsp chopped fresh marjoram, or
$^1/_2$ tsp dried marjoram
1 tsp Dijon mustard
125 g (4 oz) fresh wholemeal breadcrumbs
$^1/_2$ tsp salt
freshly grated nutmeg
freshly ground black pepper
4 sheets filo pastry, each about 45 x 30 cm (18 x 12 inches)
15 g ($^1/_2$ oz) butter

Heat the oil in a saucepan over medium heat. Add the onion and garlic and cook them for about 5 minutes, or until the onion has softened. Mix in the mushrooms, increase the heat to medium-high and cook, stirring, until the mushrooms release their juices – 3 to 4 minutes. Push the mushroom pulp to one side of the pan, then boil the juices rapidly for 5 to 10 minutes, until they have evaporated. Stir the marjoram, mustard, breadcrumbs, salt and some nutmeg and some black pepper into the mushroom pulp and set the mixture aside to cool completely.

Preheat the oven to 220°C (425°F or Mark 7). Keeping the sheets you are not using covered with a damp cloth to prevent them from drying out, lay one sheet of filo pastry on the work surface, with a long side towards you, and brush it with some melted butter. Lay another sheet of pastry on top and brush it with some more butter. Repeat with the third and fourth sheets of filo. Spoon the mushroom filling down the long side of the pastry near you, about 5 cm (2 inch) in from the edge, and pack it down lightly to form a sausage shape about 2.5 cm (1 inch) in diameter. Working away from you, roll up the filling inside the pastry. Using 2 spatulas, transfer the strudel to a large, lightly oiled baking sheet. Brush the strudel with the remaining butter and sprinkle it with some grated nutmeg. Bake for 20 to 25 minutes, until it is crisp and golden.

When cooked, leave to cool completely, then transfer to a shallow container and cover with a lid or foil.

serves 6
working time 40 mins
total time 1 hour 30 mins (inc cooling)

calories 130
total fat 5 g
saturated fat 2 g

individual tomato pizzas

250 g (8 oz) strong white flour

$^1/_4$ tsp salt

15 g ($^1/_2$ oz) butter

1 tsp dried yeast

1 tbsp safflower oil

250 g (8 oz) onions, thinly sliced

2 garlic cloves, crushed

500 g (1 lb) tomatoes, skinned and sliced

1 tbsp tomato purée

1 tbsp chopped fresh basil

1 tsp chopped fresh marjoram

90 g (3 oz) button mushrooms, sliced

freshly ground black pepper

$^1/_4$ green pepper, blanched for 2 mins

4 quail's eggs, hard boiled, sliced

1 large black olive, stoned and sliced

Sift the flour and $^1/_8$ tsp of salt into a bowl. Rub in the butter. Sprinkle on the yeast and mix thoroughly. Add sufficient warm water to form a pliable dough and knead it until smooth. Put the dough into a large oiled polythene bag and fold over the top. Set aside in a warm place to rise for about 1 hour.

Heat the oil on a pan and fry the onions and garlic gently until the onions are soft. Add the tomatoes and tomato purée and continue cooking for another 5 minutes. Add the herbs, mushrooms, the remaining salt and some freshly ground black pepper and cook until the mushrooms are soft. Set aside.

Lightly grease 4 flan tins and place on a baking sheet. Knock back the dough and knead it until it is smooth. Quarter the dough, keeping the unrolled dough cover with plastic film while you are working. Roll out each piece of dough to about 5 mm ($^1/_4$ inch) thick. Line each of the tins with a portion and spread on the cooled tomato mixture. Set aside to rise in a warm place, uncovered, for about 15 minutes, until they are puffy. Preheat the oven to 220°C (425°F or Mark 7).

Bake until the edges of the pizza are lightly browned. Garnish with green pepper, olive slivers and quail's eggs.

serves 4
working time 45 mins
total time 3 hours
(inc rising and cooling)

calories 345
total fat 9 g   saturated fat 3 g

Ultimate
budget cookbook

leek pie

1 kg (2 lb) potatoes, peeled
4 to 5 tbsp skimmed milk
75 g (2$^1/_2$ oz) Gruyere cheese, grated
freshly ground black pepper
750 g (1$^1/_2$ lb) leeks, trimmed
1 large onion, sliced
1 tbsp virgin olive oil
$^1/_4$ tsp salt
2 tsp mixed dried herbs
300 ml ($^1/_2$ pint) chicken stock
15 g ($^1/_2$ oz) butter
15 g ($^1/_2$ oz) plain flour

Cut the potatoes into quarters, then steam them until cooked – about 25 to 30 minutes. Mash them well, beat in the milk and cheese and season with pepper. Put into a large piping bag, fitted with a large star nozzle, and pipe an attractive border round the inside edge of a fireproof dish.

Cut the leeks into 1 cm ($^1/_2$ inch) thick slices. Heat the oil in a large shallow pan, and add the leeks, onion, salt and herbs. Cover the pan with a tightly fitting lid and cook gently until the leeks are just tender, shaking the pan frequently during cooking – 25 to 30 minutes. Strain the juice from the leeks and make up to 300 ml ($^1/_2$ pint) with chicken stock or milk. Set the leeks aside.

Melt the butter in the pan, add the flour, and stir in the leek juices and stock or milk. Bring to the boil, stirring all the time, until the sauce thickens. Return the leeks to the pan, reduce the heat and simmer for 5 minutes.

Brown the piped potato border under a hot grill, then pour the leeks into the centre. Serve immediately.

serves 6
working time 40 mins
total time 1 hour

calories 250
total fat 8 g
saturated fat 3 g

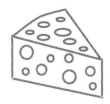

ginger stirred vegetables in pitta

2 large pittas, or 4 small pittas
1 tbsp light sesame oil
2 2.5 cm (1 inch) pieces fresh ginger, peeled
60 g (2 oz) fresh shitake mushrooms, sliced or 30 g (1 oz) dried shitake mushrooms, soaked, drained and sliced
1 small garlic clove, crushed
100 g (3^1/$_2$ oz) baby sweetcorn, sliced
250 g (8 oz) courgettes, julienned
1 tbsp fresh lemon juice
1 tsp tamari, or 1 tsp shoyu mixed with ^{1}/$_2$ tsp honey
^{1}/$_4$ tsp salt
freshly ground black pepper

Wrap the pittas in paper towels and microwave on high for 30 seconds. Cut the large pittas in half crosswise, or if using small ones, cut them open along one side. Place the oil and garlic in a wide shallow dish. Using a garlic press, squeeze the juice from one piece of ginger and shred the other piece finely. Add the ginger juice and shreds to the oil.

Microwave the oil on high for 30 seconds. Add the mushrooms to the dish, cover with plastic film, leaving a corner open, and microwave on medium for 2 minutes. Add sweetcorn, recover the dish, leaving a corner open as before, and microwave for a further 2 minutes on medium. Add the courgettes to the mushrooms and sweetcorn and microwave, uncovered, on high for one minute. Season with the lemon juice, tamari or shoyu and honey and some freshly ground black pepper, and divide the mixture among the pitta pockets.

Arrange the pittas on paper towels or a serving dish in a single layer, evenly spaced. Microwave on medium for 1^1/$_2$ minutes, rearranging the pittas halfway through. Serve at once.

serves 4
total time 20 mins

calories 165
total fat 5 g
saturated fat 1 g

hints and tips

If you prefer serve the vegetables with rice or noodles.

ULTIMATE
budget cookbook

spaghetti omelette

800 g (28 oz) canned whole
tomatoes, with their juice
125 g (4 oz) spaghetti
$^1/_2$ tsp salt
2 egg whites
125 ml (4 fl oz) semi-skimmed milk
1 tbsp chopped parsley
3 tbsp grated Parmesan cheese
freshly ground black pepper
1 tsp grated lemon rind
2 tsp virgin olive oil
60 g (2 oz) mozzarella cheese,
grated

Put the tomatoes in a pan. Simmer, stirring occasionally, until the mixture thickens – 20 to 30 minutes. Add the pasta to lightly salted boiling water. Cook the pasta until al dente – about 8 minutes. Drain the pasta and rinse it thoroughly.

In a large bowl, beat together the egg white, milk, parsley, Parmesan and a generous grinding of black pepper, the salt and lemon rind. Toss the pasta with the egg white mixture. Heat a 22 cm (9 inch) frying pan over medium-high heat. Add the oil, let it heat for about 10 seconds, then evenly coat the bottom with oil. Put half of the pasta mixture into the pan. Smooth the mixture into an even layer. Reduce the heat to medium, sprinkle the Parmesan over the pasta mixture and cover it with the remaining mixture. Let the omelette cook slowly, until it is firm and the bottom and sides are browned – about 8 minutes.

Slide the omelette onto a plate. Invert the pan over the plate and turn over both together. Cook the second side of the omelette until browned – approximately 8 minutes. While the omelette is cooking, make the sauce. Work the cooked tomatoes through a sieve, discard the seeds and warm. Slide the omelette onto a warm serving platter. Serve immediately, passing the sauce separately.

serves 8
total time 1 hour

calories 120
total fat 3 g
saturated fat 1 g

spanish omelette

2 tbsp virgin olive oil
1 onion, chopped
2 garlic cloves, chopped
2 small courgettes, trimmed and
thinly sliced
2 eggs
2 egg whites
$^1/_2$ tsp salt
freshly ground black pepper
1 large potato, peeled, cooked in
boiling water for 25 to 30 mins,
drained and coarsely chopped
125 g (4 oz) French beans, cooked
in boiling water for 5 mins, drained,
refreshed under cold running water,
and cut into 2.5 cm (1 inch) lengths
2 tomatoes, skinned seeded and
chopped
$^1/_2$ tbsp chopped fresh oregano, or
$^1/_2$ tsp dried oregano

Heat $1^1/_2$ tbsp of the oil in a frying pan over medium heat. Add the onion and fry until it is soft – about 3 minutes. Add the garlic and courgettes. Cover the pan and cook the vegetables gently for 10 minutes stirring occasionally. Remove the pan from the heat.

In a large bowl, beat together the eggs and egg whites, the salt and some freshly ground black pepper. Add the fried vegetables, the potato, beans, tomatoes, and oregano, and stir gently to mix the ingredients.

Heat the rest of the oil in a 25 cm (10 inch) frying pan, and pour in the egg mixture. Cook the omelette gently over medium heat for 3 to 4 minutes, until the underside is pale golden. Place the pan under a preheated medium-hot grill and cook the omelette until it is lightly set – 2 to 3 minutes. Cut into quarters and serve.

serves 4
working time 20 mins
total time 35 mins

calories 190
total fat 10 g
saturated fat 2 g

ULTIMATE
budget cookbook

mustard cauliflower flan

1 cauliflower, trimmed and divided
into small florets
1 tsp virgin olive oil
1 onion, finely chopped
1 large cooking apple, peeled, cored
and chopped
$1^1/_2$ tbsp Dijon mustard
2 tbsp plain flour
1 egg, lightly beaten
300 ml ($^1/_2$ pint) skimmed milk
$^1/_4$ tsp salt
white pepper
paprika

herb pastry:
125 g (4 oz) wholemeal flour
60 g (2 oz) margarine, chilled
2 tbsp finely chopped fresh
coriander
2 tbsp finely chopped flat-leaf
parsley

serves 4
working time 40 mins
total time 1 hour 30 mins

calories 330
total fat 15 g
saturated fat 4 g

Pour the flour in a bowl and rub in the margarine until the mixture resembles fine breadcrumbs. Stir in the herbs. Blend 3 to 4 tbsp of water in to the dry ingredients to form a dough. Gather the dough into a ball and knead on a floured surface until smooth. Roll out to line a flan tin 20 cm (8 inches) in diameter, and about 4 cm ($1^1/_2$ inches) deep. Prick the inside of the pastry case with a fork and chill for 30 minutes. Preheat the oven to 200°C (400°F or Mark 6). Bake for 10 to 15 minutes, until crisp. Remove from the oven and reduce the temperature to 180°C (355°F or Mark 4).

Parboil the cauliflower until tender – about 5 minutes. Drain, rinse, drain again, set aside. Heat the oil in a frying pan, add the onion and fry gently until transparent – about 3 minutes. Add the apple and cook for another 4 minutes until the apple is just tender. Spread the apple mixture inside the flan case and arrange the cauliflower on top. In a bowl, blend the mustard and flour to form a smooth paste. Whisk in the egg and then the milk, a little at a time. Add seasoning and pour into the flan case. Bake the flan for 30 to 45 minutes, until filling is set. Serve hot or cold, sprinkled with paprika.

chilli beans with cornbread topping

100 g (3^1/$_2$ oz) red kidney beans
1 tbsp safflower oil
1 onion, chopped
^{1}/$_2$ tsp chilli powder
2 garlic cloves
750 g (1^1/$_2$ lb) tomatoes, skinned
seeded and coarsely chopped
2 sticks celery, trimmed and sliced
1 tbsp tomato purée
60 g (2 oz) green olives, quartered

cornbread topping:
125 g (4 oz) cornmeal
30 g (1 oz) plain strong flour
^{1}/$_4$ tsp salt
^{1}/$_4$ tsp freshly ground black pepper
2 tsp baking powder
1 egg, beaten
125 ml (4 fl oz) skimmed milk
2 tbsp chopped parsley
30 g (1 oz) Edam cheese, finely grated

Rinse the beans. Put in a pan with cold water, covering them by 7.5 cm (3 inches). Discard the beans that float to the surface. Boil with the lid ajar for 2 minutes. Leave to soak and cool for one hour. Rinse the beans. Place in a clean pan and cover with water. Boil for 10 minutes. Rinse. Cover again with fresh water, simmer until tender – about 1 hour.

Preheat the oven to 200°C (400°F or Mark 6).

Heat the oil in a pan and fry the onion until soft. Add the chilli and garlic and fry for 1 minute. Stir in the tomatoes, peppers, celery and tomato purée. Cover, cook over medium-low heat for 10 minutes. Add the olives and beans. Cook for 5 minutes more, stirring occasionally. Divide mixture among 4 shallow dishes and set aside.

Mix the dry topping ingredients and make a well in the centre. In a separate bowl, beat together the egg, milk and parsley. Pour into the cornflour and beat until the mixture is smooth and thick. Spread over the chilli beans, sprinkle with cheese and bake until topping is firm – 15 to 20 minutes.

serves 4
working time 30 mins
total time 3 hours (inc soaking)

calories 340
total fat 10 g
saturated fat 1 g

hints and tips

If you can't find kidney beans why not try another variety.

ULTIMATE
budget cookbook

lentils with cumin and onion

350 g (12 oz) lentils, rinsed
1 tsp ground cumin
$^1/_2$ tsp salt
60 g (2 oz) brown rice
1 tbsp vegetable oil
500 g (1 lb) onions, thinly sliced
90 g (3 oz) radishes, thinly sliced
2 tbsp chopped parsley

In a large pan, bring 1.5 litres ($2^1/_2$ pints) of water to the boil. Add the lentils, cumin and salt and boil uncovered for 20 minutes. Add the rice and cook for a further 30 to 40 minutes, until the liquid has been absorbed, but the rice is still moist.

Meanwhile, heat the oil in a frying pan and fry the onions over a low heat, partially covered, until they are soft and golden brown, stirring them frequently while they are cooking – about 15 minutes.

Stir half of the fried onions into the lentils. Transfer the mixture to the centre of a shallow serving dish. Distribute the remaining onions round the lentil mixture, then arrange the radishes round the onions at the edge of the dish. Sprinkle the parsley over the lentils. Serve hot.

serves 4
working time 15 mins
total time 1 hour

calories 215
total fat 7 g
saturated fat 1 g

hints and tips

There are many lentils and pulses that you could use. Take time to try out a few.

tropical puffed pancakes

orange banana flowers with caramel sauce

plums with cream

banana crème caramel

apple sorbet with candied almonds

frozen banana yoghurt with streusel crumbs

cappuccino parfaits

peach ice cream

frozen lemon meringue torte

orange and buttermilk parfait

baked plums with streusel topping

puffy fruit omelette

The good thing about the end of the meal is that often it can be prepared well in advance so you can spend as much time as you want getting it just right!

Obviously there will be times when you'll want the end of the meal to make a real impression but on other occasions you may just want a little something to 'finish off' your food. As you'll see from the selection below, not all endings have to be dramatic. And when it comes to puds, sometimes it's the simple ones that are the best! Puddings and desserts can also provide an inexpensive, satisfying treat for the whole family. As with other foods, look out for special offers – particularly when it comes to fruit. And don't reject the idea of using tinned fruit.

For puddings they can be a great alternative – particularly when some ingredients are out of season – but unless you're required to use the juice that the fruit is canned in, be sure to drain well.

tropical puffed pancakes

3 tbsp caster sugar

$^1/_4$ tsp ground cinnamon

35 g ($1^1/_4$ oz) plain flour

30 g (1 oz) wholemeal flour

$^1/_2$ tsp baking powder

$^1/_4$ tsp salt

2 eggs, separated, plus 1 egg white

1 tbsp light or dark rum (optional)

1 tbsp safflower oil

1 lemon, grated rind only

175 ml (6 fl oz) semi-skimmed milk

2 bananas, sliced diagonally into

5 mm ($^1/_4$ inch) thick ovals

rum-pineapple topping:

300 g (10 oz) canned, unsweetened
pineapple chunks, coarsely chopped

2 tbsp dark brown sugar

2 tbsp raisins

1 lemon, juice only

2 tbsp light or dark rum (optional)

Put the pineapple into a pan and stir in the brown sugar, raisins and lemon juice. Bring to the boil then simmer for 5 minutes. Remove from the heat and stir in the rum. Keep the topping warm.

In a small bowl, mix 2 tbsp of the sugar with the cinnamon. Set aside. Preheat the oven to 220°C (425°F or Mark 7).

Sift the flours, baking powder, salt and the remaining sugar into a bowl. In a bowl, whisk the egg yolks with the rum and oil. Stir in lemon rind and milk. Whisk the flour mixture into the milk mixture to make a smooth thin batter.

Beat the egg whites until they form soft peaks. Stir half into the batter, then fold in the remainder.

Heat a 30 cm (12 inch) casserole over medium heat. Ladle the batter into the casserole, cook the pancake for 2 minutes. Top it with sliced bananas and sprinkle it with cinnamon sugar. Put into the oven until it puffs up and is golden brown – 10 to 12 minutes. Slide the pancake out of the casserole onto a warmed serving plate. Serve immediately with the rum and pineapple topping.

serves 4

working time 30 mins

total time 45 mins

calories 350

total fat 8 g

saturated fat 2 g

ULTIMATE
budget cookbook

orange banana flowers with caramel sauce

200 g (7 oz) sugar
6 oranges
2 large ripe bananas
$^1/_2$ lemon

In a small pan, combine the sugar with 6 tbsp of water. Bring to the boil, and cook it until it turns reddish-amber. Remove the pan from the heat. Standing well back to avoid being splattered, slowly pour in 4 tbsp of water. Return the pan to the heat and simmer the sauce, simmering constantly, for one minute. Transfer the caramel sauce to the fridge to cool.

While the sauce is cooling, peel and segment the oranges. Peel the bananas and slice them diagonally into pieces about 3 mm ($^1/_8$ inch) thick. Squeeze the lemon over the bananas then toss the slices to coat them with the juice.

To assemble the dessert, arrange 5 orange segments in a circle on the plate. Place a banana slice over each of the 5 points where the segments meet. Arrange 3 orange segments in a circle inside the first circle, and arrange a banana slice over each of the points where the segments meet. Top the assembly with 2 orange segments. Quarter a banana slice and arrange the quarters on top of the last two orange segments. Assemble 5 more orange banana flowers in the same way.

Just before serving, pour a little sauce around the outside of each one, letting some of the sauce fall onto the petals.

serves 6
working time 25 mins
total time 40 mins

calories 260
total fat 1 g
saturated fat 0 g

plums with cream

750 g (1¹/₂ lb) ripe purple plums,
halved and stoned
4 tbsp sugar
3 tbsp arrowroot, mixed with ¹/₄ litre
(8 fl oz) water
6 tbsp single cream

Combine the plums, sugar and the arrowroot mixture in a large pan. Bring to a simmer over a medium heat, stirring constantly. Reduce the heat to maintain a slow simmer and cover the pan. Cook the plums, stirring from time to time, until they become very soft – about 20 minutes.

Transfer the plums to a food processor or a blender and purée them. Strain the pure through a sieve into a large bowl. Ladle the purée into 6 small serving bowls. Cover the bowls and chill them for at least 30 minutes. Spoon 2 tbsp of the cream over each portion and serve.

serves 6
working time 20 mins
total time 1 hour 15 mins

calories 135
total fat 3 g
saturated fat 2 g

ULTIMATE
budget cookbook

banana crème caramel

165 g (5^1/$_2$ oz) sugar
4 tbsp fresh lemon juice
^{1}/$_4$ litre (8 fl oz) semi-skimmed milk
2 eggs
1 tbsp dark rum
1 tsp pure vanilla extract
^{1}/$_4$ tsp ground cardamom or cinnamon
^{1}/$_4$ litre (8 fl oz) puréed banana (from 2 to 3 bananas)
2 bananas, peeled and diagonally sliced

Preheat the oven to 170°C (325°F or Mark 3).

First, caramelise a 1 litre (2 pint) soufflé dish. In a small pan, combine 100 g (3^1/$_2$ oz) sugar, one tsp of the lemon juice and 3 tbsp of water. Cook over medium-high heat until the syrup browns and caramelises. Immediately remove the pan from the heat. Quickly pour the caramel into the soufflé dish. Using oven gloves, tilt the dish around to coat the bottom and about 2.5 cm (1 inch) of the sides.

For the custard, put the milk into a large pan over medium heat. As soon as it boils, remove from the heat and set it aside. Whisk the eggs with the remaining sugar, then add the rum, vanilla extract, cardamom, puréed banana and the remaining lemon juice. Stirring constantly, pour in the hot milk. Transfer to the caramelised dish.

Set the dish in a roasting pan filled with 2.5 cm (1 inch) of water. Bake until a knife inserted in the centre comes out clean. Remove from the hot water bath and cool to room temperature. Refrigerate for 2 hours. To unmould, invert a serving plate over the top of the dish and turn both over together. Garnish with banana slices before serving.

serves 6
working time 45 mins
total time 3 hours 15 mins

calories 160
total fat 2 g
saturated fat 1 g

apple sorbet with candied almonds

10 tart green apples
5 lemons, juice only
330 g (11 oz) caster sugar
30 g (1 oz) slivered almonds
1 tbsp brown sugar

Cut off and discard the top quarter of one of the apples. Using a melon baller or spoon, scoop the flesh, core and seeds from the apple, leaving a 5 mm (^{1}/4 inch) thick wall. Reserve the flesh, discard the core and seeds. Sprinkle the inside of the apple and the flesh with some of the lemon juice. Repeat with all but two of the remaining apples, then freeze the hollowed apples. Peel, seed and chop the two remaining apples and add them to the reserved flesh.

Put half a litre (16 fl oz) of water, 200 g (7 oz) of the sugar and about half the remaining lemon juice in a pan. Bring to the boil, reduce the heat to medium and simmer for 3 minutes. Add the reserved apple flesh and simmer until tender – 3 to 4 minutes. With a slotted spoon, transfer the cooked apple flesh to a blender. Discard the poaching liquid. Purée the apple, put one half litre (16 fl oz) of the purée into a bowl and allow it to cool. Stir in the remaining lemon use and sugar into the apple purée. Freeze the mixture. While the sorbet is freezing, put the slivered almonds in a small frying pan over medium heat. Toast the almonds, stirring constantly, until they turn golden brown – about 5 minutes. Stir in the brown sugar, increase the heat to high and cook the almonds until they are coated with melted sugar – about 1 minute more. Set the almonds aside. When the sorbet is firm, spoon it into the prepared apple cups, then sprinkle some candied almonds over each apple. Keep the apples in the freezer until they are served.

serves 8
working time 50 mins
total time 1–3 hours

calories 250
total fat 2 g
saturated fat 0 g

ULTIMATE
budget cookbook

frozen banana yoghurt with streusel crumbs

350 g (12 oz) ripe bananas
2 tbsp fresh lemon juice
1/2 litre (16 fl oz) plain low-fat
yoghurt
2 egg whites, at room temperature
6tbsp caster sugar
3 slices wholemeal bread
15 g (1/2 oz) butter
4 tbsp light brown sugar
1 tbsp finely chopped walnuts

Purée the bananas and lemon juice in a blender. Add the yoghurt, egg whites and caster sugar and blend the mixture for 5 minutes. Freeze the yoghurt mixture.

While the yoghurt mixture is freezing, make the streusel. Preheat the oven to 170°C (325°F or Mark 3). Tear each slice of bread into 3 or 4 pieces. Put them into a blender and process them until they are reduced to fine crumbs. Spread the crumbs in a baking tin and bake them, stirring once or twice to ensure even cooking, until crisp – about 15 minutes. Cut the butter into small bits and scatter them over the breadcrumbs. Return the pan to the oven just long enough to melt the butter. Stir the breadcrumbs to coat them with the butter, then transfer the mixture to a bowl. Stir in the brown sugar and walnuts and set the mixture aside.

When the yoghurt mixture is nearly frozen, it will still be soft. Stir in all but 2 tbsp of the streusel mixture. Return to the freezer for 15 minutes more to firm it up. Just before serving the yoghurt, sprinkle the reserved streusel over the top.

serves 8
working time 15 mins
total time 1 to 3 hours,
depending on freezing method

calories 190
total fat 3 g   saturated fat 2 g

cappuccino parfaits

1 orange, pared rind only
2 tbsp high-roast instant coffee powder
200 g (7 oz) caster sugar
4 tbsp double cream
1/2 tsp ground cinnamon
2 egg whites
cocoa powder

In a heat-proof bowl, combine the orange rind, instant coffee powder, 150 g (5 oz) of sugar and 1/2 litre (16 fl oz) of boiling water. Stir to dissolve the sugar, then let the orange rind steep for 10 minutes. Remove the rind and discard it. freeze the coffee mixture. When the mixture is frozen, divide it among 8 glass coffee cups or glasses. Freeze them.

In a small bowl, whip together the cream and cinnamon until soft peaks form. Set the mixture aside. In another bowl, beat the egg whites until they can hold soft peaks when the beater is lifted from the bowl. Continue beating, gradually adding the remaining sugar, until the whites are glossy and form stiff peaks. Fill each of the cups or glasses with some of the egg white-cream mixture. Freeze the parfaits until they are firm – about 30 minutes.

Just before serving, dust each one with some cocoa powder.

serves 8
working time 35 mins
total time 1 to 3 hours, depending on freezing method

calories 130
total fat 3 g   saturated fat 2 g

ULTIMATE
budget cookbook

peach ice cream

1 kg (2 lb) ripe peaches
1^1/$_2$ tbsp fresh lemon juice
350 g (12 oz) low-fat ricotta cheese
125 ml (4 fl oz) plain low-fat yoghurt
2 tbsp sour cream
125 ml (4 fl oz) semi-skimmed milk
75 g (2^1/$_2$ oz) light brown sugar
2 egg whites
^{1}/$_2$ tsp pure vanilla extracts
^{1}/$_4$ tsp almond extract

Bring 2 litres (3^1/$_2$ pints) of water to the boil in a large pan. Add the peaches and blanch them until their skins loosen – 30 seconds to 1 minute. Remove the peaches with a slotted spoon and set them aside. When they are cool enough to handle, peel them, cut them in half and remove the stones.

Cut enough of the peach halves into 1 cm dice to weigh about 37.5 g (13 oz). Purée the remaining peach halves with the lemon juice in a blender. Transfer the purée to a large bowl and set aside.

Put the ricotta, yoghurt and soured cream into the blender. Purée the mixture until it has a creamy consistency, stopping at least once to scrape down the sides. Blend in the milk, brown sugar, egg whites, and the vanilla and almond extracts and then whisk the mixture into the peach purée.

Stir the reserved peach dice into the purée and freeze it. If you use the food processor method of freezing, do not add the peach dice until you have processed the ice cream.

serves 8
working time 30 mins
total time 1 to 3 hours,
depending on freezing method

calories 195
total fat 5 g   saturated fat 3 g

frozen lemon meringue torte

3 lemons
250 g (8 oz) caster sugar
2 egg whites
2 tbsp cocoa powder

almond meringues:
2 egg whites
6tbsp caster sugar
75 g (2$^{1}/_{2}$ oz) blanched ground almonds
2 tbsp icing sugar

serves 8
working time 1 hour 15 mins
total time 1$^{1}/_{2}$ to 4 hours,
depending on freezing method

calories 285
total fat 5 g   saturated fat 0 g

Grate the rind from the lemons and put it into a blender or food processor. Working over a bowl to catch the juice, peel and segment one of the lemons. Squeeze the pulpy core of membranes over the bowl to extract every bit of juice. Repeat the process with the remaining lemons. To remove the seeds, strain the lemon juice into the blender. Add the lemon segments, the sugar, egg whites and 550ml (18fl oz) of water to the rind and juice, and purée the mixture.

Freeze the lemon mixture. While it is freezing, make the almond meringues.

Preheat the oven to 110°C (200°F or Mark $^{1}/_{4}$).

Line a baking sheet with greaseproof paper, or butter the sheet lightly then dust it with flour.

Beat the 2 egg whites until they form soft peaks. Beat in the sugar a tablespoon at a time. When all the sugar has been incorporated, continue beating the whites until they are glossy and hold stiff peaks. Sprinkle the ground almonds over the beaten whites and fold them in.

Fit a piping bag with a 1 cm ($^{1}/_{2}$ inch) plain nozzle, and spoon the meringue into the bag. Pipe the meringue onto the baking sheet in strips, nearly the length of the sheet. The strips should be about 2$^{1}/_{2}$ cm (1 inch) wide and 2$^{1}/_{2}$ cm (1 inch) apart. If you have no piping bag, shape the strips with a spoon. Sprinkle the strips with the icing sugar, then bake them for 1 hour.

Turn off the oven and let the strips dry with the oven door ajar for another hour. Remove the baking sheet from the oven, and gently loosen the meringues. Break the meringues into bars about 7$^{1}/_{2}$ cm (3 inches) long. When they have cooled, transfer them to an airtight container until you are ready to decorate the torte.

When the lemon sorbet is frozen, transfer it to a 20 or 23 cm (8 or 9 inch) spring-form tin. Use a rubber spatula to distribute the sorbet evenly in the tin. Rap the bottom of the tin on the work surface to collapse any large bubbles, then smooth the top with the spatula. Freeze the torte until it is firm — about 1 hour.

Remove the sides of the spring-form tin. Slide a knife or a metal spatula between the torte and the base of the tin and transfer the torte to a serving platter. Smooth the sides of the torte with a knife dipped in hot water. Press the meringue bars in place in a random pattern over the top and on the sides of the torte. The torte can be kept in the freezer with the meringue bars attached.

Just before serving, dust the torte with the cocoa powder. Put the cocoa in a sieve and tap the sieve gently as you move over the torte.

orange and buttermilk parfait

350 ml (12 fl oz) buttermilk
1/2 tbsp powdered gelatine
150 g (5 oz) sugar
2 eggs, separated, plus 1 egg white
2 tbsp frozen orange juice
concentrate, thawed
2 oranges, for garnish

Put $^1/_4$ litre (8 fl oz) of the buttermilk, the gelatine, 4 tbsp of the sugar and the egg yolks into a small pan, over low heat. Cook the mixture, stirring constantly with a wooden spoon, until it is thick enough to coat the back of the spoon – 6 to 8 minutes. Do not let the mixture come to the boil or it will curdle. Divide the mixture between 2 bowls. Whisk the remaining buttermilk into one of the bowls and whisk the orange juice concentrate into the other. Set both bowls aside at room temperature.

Make the Italian meringue. First, pour the egg whites into a deep bowl. Then set up an electric mixer – you will need to start beating the egg whites as soon as the syrup is ready.

Heat the remaining sugar with 4 tbsp of water in a small pan over medium-high heat. Boil the mixture until the bubbles rise to the surface in a random pattern, indicating that the water has nearly evaporated and the sugar is beginning to cook. With a small spoon, drop a little of the syrup into a bowl of iced water. If the syrup dissolves immediately, continue cooking. When the syrup dropped into the water can be rolled between your fingers into a supple ball, start the mixer.

serves
working time 40 mins
total time 1 hour 10 mins

calories 145
total fat 2 g
saturated fat 1 g

ULTIMATE
budget cookbook

Begin beating the egg whites at high speed. Pour the syrup into the bowl in a thin, steady stream. When all the syrup has been incorporated, decrease the speed to medium, continue beating until the egg whites are glossy, have formed stiff peaks and have cooled to room temperature. Increase the speed to high and beat the meringue for 1 minute more.

Mix a few heaped spoonfuls of the meringue into each of the buttermilk mixtures to lighten them. Fold half the remaining meringue into each mixture. Spoon the mixture containing the extra buttermilk into 8 glasses and top it with the orange mixture. Refrigerate the parfaits for at least 30 minutes.

For the garnish, segment the two oranges. Just before serving, garnish each portion with orange segments.

hints and tips

Why not try lemon or grapefruit as an alternative to orange.

baked plums with streusel topping

8 ripe purple plums, quartered and
stoned
$^1/_4$ litre (8 fl oz) brandy
4 tbsp dark brown sugar
1 orange, grated rind only

streusel topping:
4 tbsp oatmeal
4 tbsp plain flour
30 g (1 oz) butter, softened
5 tbsp dark brown sugar
4 tbsp finely chopped walnuts
1 orange, grated rind only

Arrange the plums, skin side up, in a 20 cm (8 inch) square baking dish. Preheat the oven to 200°C (400°F or Mark 6).

Combine the brandy, brown sugar and orange rind in a small pan. Bring to the boil and cook it until the liquid is reduced to 4 tbsp — about 5 minutes. Pour the syrup evenly over the plums.

To make the streusel topping, chop the oatmeal in a blender until it is as fine as flour. Transfer the chopped oatmeal to a large bowl and mix in the flour, butter, brown sugar, walnuts and rind. Dot the surface of the plums with spoonfuls of the topping. Bake the plums until the streusel has browned and the fruit juices are bubbling — 15 to 20 minutes.

serves 8
working time 30 mins
total time 45 mins

calories 185
total fat 6 g
saturated fat 2 g

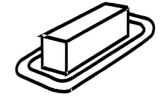

puffy fruity omelette

2 eggs, separated, plus 2 egg whites
2 tbsp plain flour
1/2 tsp baking powder
1/8 tsp salt
125 ml (4 fl oz) semi-skimmed milk
15 g (1/2 oz) caster sugar
1 red eating apple, quartered, cored
1 tsp safflower oil
1 pear, quartered, cored and cut into
1 cm (1/2 inch) pieces
1 tsp fresh lemon juice
1/4 tsp ground cinnamon
2 tbsp raspberry jam
2 tbsp unsweetened apple juice

Preheat the oven to 230°C (450°F or Mark 8).

In a bowl, whisk together the egg yolks, flour, baking powder, salt and 3 tbsp of the milk until the mixture is well blended. Whisk in the remaining milk.

In another bowl, beat the egg whites with 3tbsp of the sugar until they form soft peaks. Stir half into the yolk mixture and then fold in the remainder until the mixture is just blended. Do not over-mix. Set the egg mixture aside.

Heat the oil in a large shallow casserole over medium-high heat. Add the apple and the pear, the remaining sugar, lemon juice and the cinnamon and cook the fruit, stirring frequently, until it is tender – about 5 minutes. Remove the casserole from the heat and pour the egg mixture over the fruit. Smooth the top of the mixture. Place the casserole in the oven and bake the omelette until the top is golden-brown – 10 to 15 minutes.

While the omelette is baking, mix the raspberry jam and the unsweetened apple juice in a small dish. When the omelette is ready, dribble the syrup over it, slice into quarters and serve immediately.

serves 4
total time 40 mins

calories 200
total fat 5 g
saturated fat 1 g

Apart from tasting so good, home-made cakes are a much
cheaper alternative than the real thing.

cinnamon rock cakes

125 g (4 oz) plain flour
2 tsp baking powder
$1/2$ grated nutmeg
1 tsp ground cinnamon
125 g (4 oz) wholemeal flour
60 g (2 oz) dark brown sugar
1 lemon, finely grated rind only
60 g (2 oz) unsalted butter
90 g (3 oz) raisins
90 g (3 oz) sultanas
1 egg, beaten
2 tbsp plain low-fat yoghurt
6 tbsp skimmed milk
2 tsp caster sugar

Preheat the oven to 220°C (425°F or Mark 7). Butter and lightly flour two baking sheets.

Sift half the plain flour, baking powder, nutmeg and half of the cinnamon into the bowl. Mix in the wholemeal flour, brown sugar and lemon rind. Rub the butter into the flours until the mixture resembles fine breadcrumbs. Mix in the raisins and sultanas, and make a well in the centre. Put the egg, yoghurt and milk into the well and stir to form a fairly soft mixture.

Space heaped teaspoons of the mixture well apart on the prepared baking sheets. Bake for 15 to 20 minutes, until the cakes are well risen, golden-brown and firm to the touch. Transfer the cakes to wire racks to cool.

Mix the caster sugar with the remaining cinnamon and sprinkle over the rock cakes.

makes 16 cakes
working time 20 mins
total time 1 hour

per cake: calories 135
total fat 4 g
saturated fat 2 g

ULTIMATE
budget cookbook

grapefruit cake

125 g (4 oz) sultanas
125 g (4 oz) raisins
125 g (4 oz) currants
1 grapefruit, rind finely grated, flesh segmented and chopped
100 ml (3^1/$_2$ fl oz) fresh grapefruit juice
90 g (3 oz) margarine
90 g (3 oz) dark brown sugar
2 large eggs, beaten
175 g (6 oz) plain flour
1 tbsp clear honey

Grease the base of an 18 cm (7 inch) round cake dish and line it with greaseproof paper.

Put the sultanas, raisins, currants, grapefruit rind and juice in a bowl. Cover the fruit and microwave it on high for 3 minutes, stirring once. Remove the cover and leave the fruit to cool slightly.

Meanwhile, in another bowl, cream the margarine with the sugar and eggs until light and fluffy. Fold in the flour and the dried fruit mixture, blending well. Lastly, fold in the grapefruit flesh. Spoon the mixture into the cake dish and level the surface.

Cover the dish and place on an inverted plate in the microwave. Cook the cake on high for 10 minutes. Remove the cover, reduce the power to defrost, and cook for a further 4 to 6 minutes, or until a skewer inserted into the centre of the cake comes out clean.

Leave the cake to stand for 20 minutes before turning it out on a wire rack to cool. While the cake is still warm, brush the cake with the honey.

serves 12
working time 30 mins
total time 3 hours

calories 240
total fat 8 g
saturated fat 2 g

apple streusel slices

100 g (3^1/$_2$ oz) margarine
200 g (7 oz) wholemeal flour
750 g (1^1/$_2$ lb) dessert apples,
peeled, cored and chopped
60 g (2 oz) dark brown sugar
2 tsp ground cinnamon
90 g (3 oz) sultanas

sesame streusel:
30 g (1 oz) margarine
75 g (2^1/$_2$ oz) wholemeal flour
30 g (1 oz) Demerara sugar
1^1/$_2$ tbsp sesame seeds
1 tsp ground cinnamon

Rub the margarine into the flour in a bowl, until the mixture resembles breadcrumbs. Stir about 3 tbsp of iced water – enough to make a fairly firm dough – and knead lightly until the dough is smooth. Wrap the dough in plastic film and leave it to rest for 10 minutes.

Roll the dough out thinly on a lightly floured surface and use it to line a 30 x 20cm (12 x 8 inch) Swiss roll tin. Prick the dough with a fork and refrigerate for about 15 mins.

Meanwhile, preheat the oven 200°C (400°F or Mark 6). Put the chopped apples in a bowl with the sugar, cinnamon and sultanas and mix them together.

To make the sesame streusel, rub the margarine into the flour, until the mixture resembles breadcrumbs. Stir in the sugar, sesame seeds and cinnamon. Sprinkle 3 tbsp of the mixture over the dough in the tin to absorb the juice from the apples. Spread the apple mixture in the tin, sprinkle the remaining streusel over the apples. Bake for 30 to 35 minutes, until the streusel in golden-brown. Cut the cake into slices when it has cooled.

serves 20
working time 40 mins
total time 2 hours

calories 135
total fat 5 g
saturated fat 1 g

frosted orange cake

300 g (10 oz) plain flour
2½ tsp baking powder
125 g (4 oz) margarine
90 g (3 oz) light brown sugar
2 oranges, grated rind only
2 eggs
3 tbsp fresh orange juice

orange glacé icing:
125 g (4 oz) icing sugar
3tbsp fresh orange juice
½ orange, grated rind only

Preheat the oven to 175°C (325°F or Mark 3). Line an 18 cm (10 inch) round cake tin with greaseproof paper.

Sift the flour and baking powder together into a bowl and rub in the margarine until the mixture resembles fine breadcrumbs. Mix in the sugar and orange rind. In another bowl, beat the eggs and fresh orange juice together, then mix them into the dry ingredients with a wooden spoon. Turn the batter into the tin and level the top. Bake the cake for about 1 hour, until well risen and firm to the touch. A skewer inserted into the centre of the cake should come out clean. Turn the cake onto a wire rack. Leave it until cool, then peel off the paper.

To make the icing, sift the icing sugar into a bowl and beat in just enough of the orange juice to give a thick coating consistency. Spread the icing over the top of the cake, allowing it to run down the sides in places. Sprinkle the icing with the grated orange rind and leave the cake until the icing has set.

serves 14
working time 25 mins
total time 3 hours 30 mins

calories 214
total fat 7 g
saturated fat 2 g

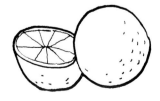

upside-down apple ring

4 digestive biscuits, crushed

2 dessert apples, peeled, cored and sliced

125 g (4 oz) margarine

90 g (3 oz) dark brown sugar

2 egg whites, lightly beaten

150 ml ($^1/_4$ pint) plain low-fat yoghurt

250 g (8 oz) wholemeal flour

1 tsp baking powder

1 tbsp ground mixed spice

1 cooking apple, peeled, cored and grated

Grease a 22 cm (9 inch) flat-based tube mould and sprinkle it with the biscuit crumbs to coat its inner surface. Arrange the apple slices in the base of the mould, overlapping them slightly.

In a large bowl, cream the margarine and the sugar, egg whites and yoghurt. Sift in the flour with the baking powder and mixed spice, adding the bran left in the sieve. Fold the dry ingredients and the grated apple into the creamed mixture. Spoon the batter into the prepared ring mould and spread it evenly.

Microwave on medium high for 8 to 10 minutes, giving the dish a quarter turn every two minutes. The cake is cooked when it feels springy to the touch. Leave it to stand for 5 minutes before turning it out. Serve the apple ring warm or cold.

serves 12
working time 20 mins
total time 35 mins

calories 215
total fat 10 g
saturated fat 2 g

hints and tips

If serving warm, why not top with custard.

genoese sponge

3 eggs
1 egg white
90 g (3 oz) caster sugar
125 g (4 oz) plain flour
30 g (1 oz) butter, melted and cooled slightly

Preheat the oven to 180°C (355°F or Mark 4). Butter a 30 x 20 x 4 cm (12 x 8 x 1^1/$_2$ inch) rectangular tin and line the base with greaseproof paper.

Put the eggs, egg white and caster sugar into a mixing bowl. Set the bowl over a saucepan of hot, but not boiling, water on a low heat. Using a hand-held electric mixer, whisk the eggs and sugar together until thick and very pale. Remove the bowl from the pan and continue whisking until the mixture is cool and falls from the whisk in a ribbon trail. Sift the flour very lightly over the surface of the egg and sugar mixture, then fold it in gently, using a large metal spoon. Gradually fold in the melted butter.

Pour the sponge batter into the prepared tin and spread it evenly. Bake it for 25 to 30 minutes, until well risen, springy to the touch and very slightly shrunk from the sides of the tin. Carefully unmould the sponge onto a wire rack. Loosen the paper but do not remove it. place another wire rack on top of the paper then invert both racks together so that the sponge is right side up on top of the paper. Remove the top rack and allow the sponge to cool.

makes one 30 x 20cm sponge
working time 20 mins
total time 1 hour

calories 175
total fat 9 g
saturated fat 2 g

hints and tips

This can be served as a dessert or just eaten with tea and coffee.

caraway seed sponge

3 eggs, separated
150 g (5 oz) light brown sugar
125 g (4 oz) plain flour
1 tsp baking powder
1$\frac{1}{2}$ tsp cornflour
2 tsp margarine
1 tbsp orange juice (optional)
1 tsp caraway seeds
icing sugar to decorate

Preheat the oven to 200°C (400°F or Mark 6). Grease a 20 cm (8 inch) round cake tin or a petal cake tin approximately 18 cm (7 inches) in diameter. Line the tin with greaseproof paper.

Whisk the egg whites until they stand firm in peaks. Gradually stir in the brown sugar, 1 tbsp at a time, then quickly fold in the egg yolks. Sift the flour, baking powder and cornflour together two or three times into another bowl, to aerate them thoroughly. Heat the margarine in a small pan until it melts, then remove the pan from the heat and add the orange juice and 2 tbsp of water. Using a metal spoon or rubber spatula, fold the flour mixture quickly and evenly into the cake mixture, followed by the melted mixture and the caraway seeds. Pour the batter into the prepared tin and bake, until well risen, golden-brown and firm to the touch — 25 to 30 minutes in the round tin, or 30 to 40 minutes in the petal tin.

Turn the cake out onto a wire rack and leave it to cool, then remove the paper. Before serving the cake, sift icing sugar lightly over the top.

serves 12
working time 25 mins
total time 3 hours 30 mins

calories 125
total fat 3 g
saturated fat 0 g

cook's glossary

Sometimes the most confusing part of preparing food can be working out what the instructions mean. Cooks and cookery writers can use some terms so regularly that they can forget that, for those new to cooking, the names just add confusion and make you feel even more worried about following any recipe with any element of success. That's why we've included some common cookery terms plus an explanation as to what they mean.

al dente	Italian term, used to describe food, mainly pasta, that has been cooked to the point where it still has a slight resistance when you bite into it.
to baste	to stop meat, fish and poultry drying out, you keep the food moist by spooning over the liquid that it's cooking in.
to bind	this basically means that you need to make sure ingredients are well mixed so that all the ingredients are well blended and appear as one consistency.
to blanch	this involves putting the particular ingredient into a pan filled with cold water, brought to the boil, and then the water is discarded.
to chop	to cut into small pieces.
to coat	to cover e.g. you may be asked to coat, or cover, fish or chicken in breadcrumbs.
to cook in foil	vegetables, as well as portions of fish, or chicken, can be cooked in a 'parcel' of silver foil. This can take a little longer than other methods but it helps retain nutrients (vitamins and minerals) and taste, needs only a little liquid, if any, and helps cut down on the washing up!
to cream	this involves mixing the ingredient, or ingredients, until they are creamy in consistency.

to curdle	this is what you try to avoid doing! It happens when ingredients separate and won't blend in. It can be a problem if you're making a sauce, for example, and you add the liquid too quickly to a flour and fat base. It can also happen when adding eggs to a mixture.
to dice	cut into small, even pieces.
to fold	to mix one ingredient into another, gently, with either a spatula or metal spoon.
to glaze	this involves brushing, with a pastry brush, either milk, egg, or sugar based liquid to food before cooking so as to give a 'shine'. Often used on pastry.
julienne	thin matchstick sized vegetables, or orange, lemon or lime rind.
to parboil	to cook for a short time in boiling water: often potatoes are parboiled before roasting as it cuts cooking time.
to poach	this requires you to cook food in simmering liquid (see below)
purée	to mash or sieve to a smooth consistency, can also be done in a food processor.
rub in	when you make pastry you 'rub in' the margarine, or butter, and flour lightly with your fingers until the mixture turns into breadcrumbs
to sauté	basically means shallow frying, where you use just a little oil.
to season	to add salt and pepper, although seasoning often comes down to taste so amounts do not need to be followed rigidly. Also experts advise that we cut down on salt (see below) so it's always better to start with a little and add slowly rather than end up with too much.
to simmer	this is when something being cooked in liquid is left on the hob, or stove, on a low light, at a consistent temperature. For example, soups, sauces and stews. An occasional bubble will make sure that the food is still cooking but it's important that you avoid letting the food bubble furiously as it can burn rather than cook! Simmering can also be used for reheating, for example, tinned soups.

to steam   this is when food is cooked by the steam that rises from the water rather than by the liquid itself. Steaming is a particularly good way of cooking vegetables as it helps retain their nutrients (vitamins and minerals) as well as their flavour. You don't need to buy a dedicated steamer to steam food. You can use a wire expanding metal basket (available at hardware stores and kitchen departments) or a flameproof dish placed above a pan, with a little water, and covered. Keep checking the water though to make sure the pan doesn't dry out.

to stew   to cook something slowly in a saucepan or casserole, by simmering in some liquid, but covered with a lid. Often cooked in the oven. Stewing meat, for example, means that the food will cook through thoroughly but will also remain moist and soft.

stir frying   this traditional Chinese way of cooking is a healthy as well as tasty way of serving up food. The idea is that finely cut vegetables and/or meat, chicken or fish or cooked on a high heat, very quickly in a little oil. You need to watch the food though — and keep stirring — to make sure everything is evenly cooked — and doesn't burn!

UK/US glossary
of foods, utentsils and terms

FOOD

aubergine	eggplant
beetroot	beet
broad beans	fava beans
chickpeas	garbanzo beans
chips	French fries
coriander	cilantro
cornflour	cornstarch
courgette	zucchini
crisps	potato chips
double cream	heavy cream
French beans	green beans
haricot beans	navy beans
mangetout	snowpeas
marrow	squash
mature cheese	sharp cheese
pepper	bell pepper
pitta bread	pocket bread
plain flour	all-purpose flour
pulses	legumes
rocket	arugula
runner beans	string beans

ULTIMATE
budget cookbook

single cream	light cream
spring onions	scallions
sultanas	golden raisins
swede	rutabaga
sweetcorn	corn
unsalted butter	sweet butter

UTENSILS AND TERMS

baking tray	cookie sheet
barbeque	grill
frying pan	skillet
grill	broil
puree	paste
sieve	strainer

ULTIMATE
budget cookbook

ULTIMATE
budget cookbook